Test Yourself in

CONTRACT

Test Yourself in

CONTRACT

John Hamer
LLB (Hons), FATC

Carolyn Naughton
LLB (Hons), Solicitor

&

Max Young
BA (Business Law) (Hons), MA (Business Law),
MPhil, MITD

Series Editor: Adrian Keane, Barrister,
Reader, ICSL

BLACKSTONE
PRESS LIMITED

First published in Great Britain 1997 by Blackstone Press Limited,
9–15 Aldine Street, London W12 8AW.   Telephone: 0181-740 2277

© J. Hamer, C. Naughton and M. Young, 1997

ISBN: 1 85431 630 3

British Library Cataloguing in Publication Data
A CIP catalogue record for this book is available from the British
Library.

Typeset by Style Photosetting Limited, Mayfield, East Sussex
Printed by Bell and Bain Limited, Glasgow

CONTENTS

FOREWORD

This book has been prepared by senior teaching staff of the Department of Law at the University of Luton. Its purpose is to meet the needs of students studying contract law on LLB and combined law degree courses although it is also suitable for students studying contract law on business studies and CPE courses.

This publication will be revised regularly to keep it up-to-date and to improve its content based on the benefit of experience and comments made by readers. Comments are always welcome and may be addressed either to the authors or the publishers.

John Hamer
Carolyn Naughton
Max Young

April 1997

INTRODUCTION

PLEASE DO NOT ATTEMPT, OR EVEN READ, THE MULTIPLE CHOICE TEST QUESTIONS CONTAINED IN THIS BOOK UNTIL YOU HAVE READ THIS INTRODUCTION!

A. THE PURPOSE OF THE MULTIPLE CHOICE TESTS

It must be rare, on opening a book and turning to its first page, to be greeted by such a command, albeit a polite command. However, there is a very good reason for such a command: that if you do embark upon testing yourself in the law of contract by using the Multiple Choice Tests (MCTs) in this book, *before* you have read the following few pages on: (a) the purpose of the MCTs, (b) the nature and format of the MCTs, (c) popular misconceptions and (d) advice on taking the tests, then it is likely that you will simply defeat the purpose of this book.

The MCTs contained in this book have two purposes. The first is to enable you to test, with speed and accuracy, whether you have a sound working knowledge and comprehension of the main principles of law and the leading cases in the law of contract. The MCT questions used are directed at the general rules, the principal exceptions to those rules and the leading authorities. Wherever possible, they concentrate on the modern law and important decisions. They are not directed at narrow, antiquated, abstruse or esoteric points that a practitioner, or even a scholar, might properly need to look up and research. This explains why, as we shall see, each question has to be answered in only $2\frac{1}{2}$ minutes.

The second purpose is to enable you, after the test, to look at the answers which have been provided and to identify, with precision, your weaknesses and the gaps in your knowledge and understanding, so that you can revisit these areas and take appropriate remedial action.

B. THE NATURE AND FORMAT OF THE MCTs

This book contains two MCTs, MCT1 and MCT2 which together cover most subjects normally found in the syllabus for undergraduate courses in the law of contract.

Each of the MCTs comprises 60 questions, to be taken at one sitting. The 60 questions set have to be answered in no more than 2½ hours. This means that if you divide the time equally between the questions, you will have 2 minutes and 30 seconds to answer each question.

Format

The questions in the MCTs contained in this book are always accompanied by four possible answers: [A], [B], [C] and [D]. You are required to select just one answer, the one that you think is correct/the best.

The questions often take the form of a factual problem and conclude with a specific question, such as 'On these facts, what is the most appropriate advice to give to the client?' or 'On these facts, which of the following orders is the judge most likely to make?' Questions of this kind are designed to test whether you are able to recognise the law appropriate to the given facts and/or whether you are able to apply the law to the facts and thereby identify the correct outcome.

Other questions take the form of a number of legal propositions, only one of which is correct or, as the case may be, incorrect, or they ask about a specific point of law. Thus as to the former, the question may read, 'Which of the following propositions is correct?' or 'Which of the following propositions is INCORRECT?' As to the latter, the question may state a rule of law and then conclude, for example, 'Which of the following is NOT an exception to this general rule?'. Questions of this kind are designed to test your knowledge of the law.

Some questions combine both a factual scenario and a choice of legal propositions so that, after setting out the facts, the question may read, for example, 'Which of the following best describes the principles which the court should apply to these facts?'

C. MCTs – POPULAR MISCONCEPTIONS

MCTs are easier than traditional examinations

This view tends to be expressed by those who have never attempted an MCT. Multiple choice tests are not easier – they are different. The experience of students who have taken MCTs, both at home and overseas, is that such tests are, in their own way, much more demanding than traditional examinations. There are three principal reasons for this.

First, MCTs typically cover the whole syllabus. If you have been brought up on conventional examinations and have adopted the 'question-spotting' approach, the MCT obviously comes as a very nasty shock!

Secondly, the MCT offers no scope for the student who would waffle. In conventional examinations, some students, unaware or not too sure of the correct answers, will hedge their bets, setting out at length all such seemingly relevant legal knowledge as they possess, but making no real effort to apply the law, simply skirting around the central issues with deliberate equivocation. There is no scope for such tactics in the MCT: faced with four competing answers, only one of which is correct, you must nail your colours to the mast.

Thirdly, there is the obvious pressure that comes from having to answer some 60 questions at the rate of $2\frac{1}{2}$ minutes per question. This calls for the ability to analyse, digest and comprehend material at speed, before reaching a firm conclusion, only to move on to repeat the exercise in the next question, and so on.

MCT means multiple guess

It is perfectly accurate to say that if you attempt an MCT in which each question has four competing answers, then by the law of averages you *can* score 25%. Sensible students, however, do not approach MCTs in the same way that they approach the national lottery. (In the real world even if they did, it would be of little assistance – the passmark is usually more than double 25%. On the Bar Vocational Course, for example, a student who answers correctly 60% of all the questions set (in the MCT in civil evidence and procedure or criminal evidence and procedure), will achieve a bare pass; and in many jurisdictions the percentage required to pass is much higher.) Further information is given below on how to mark and rate your performance in the MCTs in this book.

MCTs are inferior to traditional tests and examinations

The validity of this criticism depends upon what one is seeking to test or examine. Obviously the MCT is not an appropriate tool to test oral legal skills such as advocacy or negotiation, just as it would be an inappropriate means of testing the practical skills of a pianist or an airline pilot. Equally, it cannot test your *creative* legal powers, whether in writing a legal essay or answering a legal problem (although it is interesting to note, in passing, that there is a high degree of correlation between student results in MCTs and in other forms of testing which do involve oral performances and written work). However, experience shows that the MCT is an excellent vehicle for testing, with accuracy, levels of knowledge and comprehension and the power of legal analysis, in particular the ability to recognise the law appropriate to any given set of facts, to apply that law and thereby to identify the correct outcome.

MCTs cannot test the 'grey areas'

This is simply incorrect! For every 'grey area' question, there can be a suitably 'grey area' answer. For example, if on a particular point the authorities conflict, the correct answer may simply read, 'The authorities are in conflict on this point'. (Note, however, that such wording may also be used for an incorrect answer, i.e. in a question where the authorities are not in conflict at all.) Another possibility, in 'grey areas', is to build a question around the facts of an important reported case, thereby testing whether you know of, and have understood, that case. That said, it is certainly true that it can be more demanding to set good MCT questions on 'grey areas', and for this reason they tend to be avoided, unless they concern an important area of the law.

D. ADVICE ON TAKING THE TESTS

The purpose of the MCTs in this book is likely to be defeated unless you observe certain basic rules.

1. Do not attempt an MCT until you have completed your studies in the subjects covered

The MCTs in this book are designed to be taken only *after* you have completed your studies in the subject areas covered and *before* you are formally examined in them.

2. Take the MCT under examination conditions

Make sure that you will have an *uninterrupted* period of $2\frac{1}{2}$ hours in which to complete *the whole test*. Also, remove from the room any relevant books or materials that you might be tempted to use – the MCTs are to be taken without access to books and materials.

3. Observe the time limits

Observe the overall time limit of $2\frac{1}{2}$ hours and try to spend no longer than an average of $2\frac{1}{2}$ minutes on each question. You will doubtless find that some of the questions can be answered in less time, whereas others require slightly more time – the questions vary in length and difficulty. However, the overall time limit reflects the standard of the MCT as a whole, and should not be exceeded.

4. Read all four competing answers to each question before making a selection

Whether a question is a problem-type question or a propositions-type one, you should *always* look at all four competing answers before making a selection. There are three good reasons for doing so.

First, an answer may refer to another answer or answers. For example, the question may set out a judge's ruling on a particular point of law, and conclude, 'Which of the following reasons could justify the judge's ruling?' [A] may then set out one reason and suggest that this *alone* could justify the ruling; [B] may set out a different reason and suggest that this *alone* could justify the ruling; and [C] may read, 'The reasons in both [A] and [B]'.

Secondly, even when you are relatively confident that you know the correct answer before you even look at the options on offer, and you are therefore tempted simply to select the 'correct' answer and to ignore the other answers, reading those other answers to check that they are indeed incorrect is the best way of confirming your initial selection.

Thirdly, there may well be occasions when you are unsure as to the correct answer. In these circumstances, it is often possible to identify the correct answer by the process of eliminating others which you know to be incorrect. Often you will find that the question-setter has included one answer which although somewhat plausible is clearly incorrect, and another which is also incorrect, although not quite so obviously, thereby reducing the effective choice from four to two – the two remaining answers will test whether you have understood the legal principle in question.

5.   Deem the question-setter infallible

If your initial reaction, on reading a particular question and the four competing answers, is that you need more factual information before you can select the correct answer, or that there are two correct answers, or that the correct answer seems to have been omitted, quickly swallow your pride and re-read the question to see if there is something which you have missed or the importance of which you failed to take note on the first reading. If, having re-read the question and answers, you remain convinced that you need more information, or that there are two correct answers, or no correct answer, then select the answer which, in your opinion, gets nearest to being correct or is the best from which you have to make a choice.

6.   Mark your performance

After you have completed each MCT – and probably after a break of a suitable length – you will want to mark your performance. You will find the correct answers to MCT 1 and MCT 2 listed in Appendix 1 and Appendix 2, respectively. Award yourself one mark for each question that you have answered correctly. If you have selected one of the other three answers to the question, selected more than one answer or not made a selection at all, you should *not* subtract a mark – you simply gain no mark for that question. You may then rate your overall performance according to the following table.

Number of questions answered correctly in MCT1 / MCT2	Comment
0–35	A performance ranging from the awful to the weak. At best, on 35, you are showing insufficient knowledge and comprehension in over 40% of all subjects tested.
36–44	A performance ranging from one of bare competence to competence. You are showing insufficient knowledge and comprehension in 26–40% of all subjects tested.
45–53	A performance ranging from the competent to the very competent. You are showing insufficient knowledge and comprehension in 11–25% of all subjects tested.
54–60	A performance ranging from the very competent to the outstanding. You are showing insufficient knowledge and comprehension in only 10% or less of all subjects tested.

7. Review your performance

After you have marked your performance, take a break! You need to be fully refreshed before you embark upon the most important part of the exercise, namely the review of your performance by reference to the note-form answers to the questions of MCT 1 and MCT 2, which you will find in Appendix 3 and Appendix 4, respectively. Thorough review is important because it allows you to identify with precision the gaps in your knowledge and understanding of the law with a view to further work or revision.

Look at *all* of the written answers, not just those to the questions which you got wrong. By looking at the answers to the questions which you answered correctly, you will usually confirm your understanding of the law. Sometimes, however, you may discover that although your answer was in fact correct, your reasoning was defective. Equally, you need to know the reasons for the answers as to which you could only make an inspired guess.

MCT1

[TIME LIMIT: 2½ HOURS]

1. Which of the following is NOT an invitation to treat?

[A] An advertisement which states that an auction will be 'without reserve'.
[B] A display of goods in a shop window marked 'Special Offer'.
[C] Goods offered for sale in a newspaper.
[D] An application form for hire purchase.

2. Lisa wants to sell her grandfather clock. She writes the following letter to four people: 'Dear X, In the past you have shown an interest in my grandfather clock. I have decided to sell my clock; if you are interested in making an offer please send me a bid by first-class post to reach me no later than 3 p.m. on the 15th of this month. I am writing the same letter to four people.' James sends in the highest bid. After considering the bids Lisa rejects them all and accepts instead an offer from Tony, a work colleague who offered her £200 more than James. Which of the following is correct?

[A] The letter requesting the bids is an invitation to treat and Lisa can accept or reject any bid.
[B] The letter requesting the bid is an invitation to treat but Lisa has a contractual duty to accept a bid only from the four invited.
[C] The letter requesting the bids is an offer and Lisa has a duty to accept the highest bid.
[D] The letter requesting the bids is an offer and Lisa must chose to accept one of the four bids.

3. Peter offered a substantial commission to Mary, an estate agent, if she found 'a client who purchased' his house. Mary went to great trouble to advertise the house and found someone who was prepared to buy Peter's house for the asking price. However, at the last moment Peter decided not to sell his house. Which of the following situations best represents Mary's position?

[A] She is entitled to the full commission as she had found a buyer who is still prepared to purchase the house at Peter's asking price.

[B] She is not entitled to any commission since she has not done that which was required of her because Peter has not sold his house.

[C] She is entitled to compensation for loss of the chance to earn the commission.

[D] She is entitled to compensation for the expenditure she wasted.

4. Zelda offers to sell Velma a car for £1,500. Consider which of the following situations DO NOT destroy Zelda's offer.

(i) Velma asks if hire purchase is available to help her buy the car.

(ii) Velma asks Zelda if she would consider selling the car for £1,200 but that if she is not willing to sell it for £1,200 then she, Velma, would still like the chance to buy the car for £1,500.

(iii) Velma agrees to buy the car for £1,500 if Zelda fits a CD player in the car.

[A] (i) and (ii).
[B] (ii) and (iii).
[C] (i) and (iii).
[D] All of them.

5. Eric, who lost his dog, placed a notice outside his house which read 'Reward – £20 to anyone who returns my dog to me'. Fred, who had already found the dog, read the notice and immediately returned the dog to Eric. Eric, who had had second thoughts, said to Fred 'Thanks for the dog. I'll give you £5 for your trouble'. Fred protested that this was not enough and Eric now refuses to give Fred either the £20 or the £5. Which of the following statements is correct?

[A] Fred is entitled to the £20 because he returned the dog to Eric.
[B] Fred is only entitled to the £5 because he did not know of the reward when he found the dog.
[C] Fred is not entitled to either the £20 or the £5.
[D] Fred is entitled to be paid a reasonable sum based on the *quantum meruit* basis because he returned the dog to Eric at Eric's request.

6. Carolyn made an offer to sell her car to Max for £1,000. She left the message on Max's fax machine at home. Max accepted the offer by leaving a message on her fax machine at home. Unfortunately Carolyn's son Peter thought the fax machine paper was for him to use. He tore the message off the machine and played with it and the *au pair* put the paper in the bin. Unaware of the acceptance Carolyn sold the car to John. Max has arrived to collect the car. Is there a contract?

[A] No. Carolyn is not bound by Max's acceptance because it was not communicated to her.
[B] Yes. Carolyn is bound by the acceptance because she should have taken reasonable steps to prevent her son from destroying the message.
[C] No. Carolyn is not bound because a fax machine is not a recognised instrument to make contracts on.
[D] None of the above.

7. On 1 April Anne offers to sell her caravan to Gladys for £3,500. Anne says to Gladys that she can have 3 weeks to consider the offer but that she must have notice in writing if she wants to buy the caravan. Ten days later Gladys sends a letter of acceptance to Anne by recorded delivery. The letter is lost when a dishonest postal worker steals the letter. Not having heard from Gladys, Anne decides not to sell the caravan afterall since she has now found out it is worth £5,000. Gladys now wants the caravan. Which of the following statements is correct?

[A] There is a contract between Gladys and Anne because a contract came into existence when the letter of acceptance was posted.
[B] The offer has been revoked because Anne has decided not to sell the caravan after all.
[C] There is no contract because Anne never received the letter.
[D] There is a contract between Gladys and Anne because although the letter was never received by Anne it was sent by recorded delivery and Gladys can prove that she posted it.

8. In relation to the rule concerning communication of acceptance by telephone which of the following statements is correct?

[A] An acceptance takes affect when the offeree speaks into the telephone.
[B] An acceptance takes affect when the offeree speaks into the telephone even if the offeror does not actually hear the words of acceptance.
[C] An acceptance only takes affect when it is heard by the offeror.
[D] An acceptance only takes affect when it is heard by the offeror and the offeror tells the offeree that he understands the message.

9. Jardines, a firm of solicitors, acted for Chris who was buying a new house from Jerry Builders Ltd. Under the terms of the contract the builders had to give notice when the house was ready for Chris to move in. Payment for the house had to be made on the same day. The notice period was 10 days. In the construction industry it was usual to send such notices by first-class post to the buyer's solicitors. The builders left a message on Jardines' answering machine. The message stated that this was the formal notice requesting payment and allowing Chris to move in. The notice gave the required 10 days' notice. Unfortunately a new administrator at Jardines wiped the answering machine tape clean before it was heard. No further communication was made by the builders until the anticipated day of payment arrived. By this time it was too late for Jardines to arrange the transfer of moneys to the builders. Chris's moving day was delayed and the builders are demanding interest for late payment. Jardines are denying liability because such notices are usually sent in writing by post. Which of the following statements is correct?

[A] Jardines are liable for the interest because they did not act upon the notice received by their offices.

[B] The contract is silent on the method of communication of the notice. Therefore the notice can be communicated by an answering machine.

[C] Jardines is a commercial organisation and therefore is expected to act upon messages received in whatever form in a proper manner.

[D] Such notices are usually in writing and sent by post. It would be unreasonable for Jardines to be bound by a message on an answering machine unless it had been expressly stipulated.

10. Phil takes his car into a garage to have its 6,000 mile service. On returning to collect his car he is taken aback when he is presented with a bill for £260. The bill is made up of £60 for the service, £120 for the replacement of two tyres whose tread was below the legal limit and £80 for a modification to rectify a design fault to the car which made it unsafe to drive. How much does Phil have to pay?

[A] £60 for the service.
[B] £140 for the service and the modification.
[C] £180 for the service and the tyres.
[D] £260 for all the items on the bill.

11. Andy advertises his horse for sale for £800 in a local newspaper. Katy phones Andy and tells him that his horse is just the thing that she has be looking for but that she will not be able to inspect it for a week. Andy says that if he gets a buyer before then he will have to let the horse go. Katy says that if Andy agrees not to sell the horse for a week she will give him £50: Andy agrees. What have Andy and Katy agreed?

[A] The sale of the horse for £50.
[B] That Andy will not sell his horse to anyone else for a week.
[C] That Andy will only sell his horse to Katy.
[D] Nothing.

12. For what reason did the plaintiff in *Williams v Roffey Bros and Nicholls (Contractors) Ltd* [1990] 1 All ER 512 qualify for the extra payment?

[A] Williams had done more than he was contractually obliged to do.
[B] Roffey Bros's promise did not require Williams to do anything to show extra consideration.
[C] Roffey Bros received the benefit of not having to pay a penalty.
[D] Roffey Bros was estopped from denying Williams' right to this payment.

13. Which of the following is FALSE at common law as regards the formation of a contract?

[A] Past consideration is no consideration.
[B] Consideration must be adequate but need not be real.
[C] Consideration must move from the promisee.
[D] Nominal consideration is real consideration.

14. Rowan sells her Hornby train layout to Paul for £2,000. She delivered the train layout to Paul and told him she would accept £1,500 as she no longer had the necessary space for the layout. Paul in exchange for this promise offers his stamp collection valued at £50. Can Rowan now change her mind and demand the outstanding balance of £500?

[A] No, because the rule in *Pinnel's Case* clearly states that the payment of less than the agreed amount outstanding if supported by an independent benefit can discharge a debt.

[B] Yes, because Rowan and Paul have not reached adequate accord and satisfaction because £1,500 cannot discharge the debt of £2,000.

[C] Yes, because Paul has not fully discharged the original contract.

[D] No, because a new contract has come into being.

15. Which of the following is NOT a correct statement in relation to promissory estoppel?

[A] There must be a pre-existing contractual relationship between the parties.

[B] Promissory estoppel is a form of consideration.

[C] Promissory estoppel cannot be used to found a cause of action.

[D] The effect of promissory estoppel is usually to suspend the rights of the party who has agreed to forgo their strict legal rights.

16. Jodie owns a four bedroomed house. She lets one of the rooms to David for £50 per week. David started having financial difficulties and Jodie agreed to reduce the rent to £40 until his financial affairs improved. That was 6 months ago and Jodie is now in financial difficulty. She would now like David to start paying £50 again immediately and recover the balance of the £50 weekly rent for the past 6 months. David is refusing but will agree to paying £50 a week in a month's time. What is Jodie entitled to?

[A] Jodie is only entitled to £40 per week since the agreement was amended.

[B] Jodie is entitled to £50 per week in a month's time.

[C] Jodie is entitled to the £50 per week straight away.

[D] Jodie is entitled to the £50 per week immediately and the balance of the £50 for the past 6 months.

17. Philipa owes Erica, a car dealer, £25,000 for a car she bought from Erica last month. Philipa has the money to pay Erica but before the time is due for payment Erica wins £8,000,000 on the National Lottery. Erica is obviously overjoyed by her good fortune and tells Philipa to forget the debt and to enjoy the money on a good time. Philipa has now spent the £25,000. Unfortunately Erica could not find her winning ticket and is desperate for the £25,000 which she demands back from Philipa. Which of the following statements is correct?

[A] Since Philipa paid Erica no money she did not provide any consideration for Erica's promise to forgo the £25,000 and therefore Erica is entitled to have the £25,000 back.

[B] Since Philipa did not ask Erica to forgo the £25,000 Erica is entitled to have the £25,000 back.

[C] In the circumstances it is not inequitable for Erica to go back on her word and she is therefore entitled to have her £25,000 back.

[D] Erica will have to bear her sad loss and will be estopped from demanding the £25,000 back.

18. Peter, who was considering buying a computer for his business, approached Smart Accounts Ltd who supplied 'world class' leading edge accounting software. Smart Accounts Ltd assured Peter that their software would go like a bomb on Brill Computers Ltd's 2,000 series PC. Smart Accounts Ltd said that they did not supply their software direct to the public but if Peter purchased a Brill 2,000 PC together with their software from Brill Computers Ltd they would guarantee and maintain the software 'for life'. Reassured by this Peter purchased a Brill 2,000 PC together with Smart Accounts Ltd's software. The software has proved to be a total disaster and Smart Accounts Ltd have refused to honour their guarantee and maintain the software telling Peter to take his complaints to Brill Computers Ltd; unfortunately Brill Computers Ltd have gone into liquidation leaving no assets. Which of the following statements is correct?

[A] Peter has no remedy since he did not buy the software from Smart Accounts Ltd and there is no point in suing Brill Computers Ltd since they have no assets.

[B] Peter can sue Smart Accounts Ltd since Brill Computers Ltd acted as their agent in the sale of the software.

[C] Peter can sue Brill Computers Ltd for breach of contract.

[D] Peter can sue Smart Accounts Ltd for breach of contract.

19. What is the doctrine of privity of contract?

[A] Only parties to a contract can sue or be sued under that contract.
[B] Any person who has a benefit under a contract can sue upon it.
[C] Any person seeking protection under the contract can rely upon it.
[D] It protects the privacy of the parties to the contract.

20 Tony made a contract with John to arrange the catering for his daughter's wedding reception. The night before the wedding John contacts Tony informing him that he is double booked and is unable to provide any of the catering. Tony was unable to find a replacement at such short notice. This meant the wedding reception consisted of a few home-made sandwiches and wine. Not even the cake was provided. Tony and his family, especially the daughter, were distraught. Can Tony claim any damages?

[A] No. Tony cannot claim any damages because the courts will not award damages for loss of pleasure and disappointment.
[B] Yes, but Tony can only recover damages for his own disappointment and loss of pleasure he cannot recover damages for his family's loss of pleasure.
[C] Yes. The court will award damages to Tony and his family.
[D] Yes. Tony can recover damages for his disappointment and loss of pleasure which will include an amount for seeing his family disappointed.

21. Carol has not spoken to her sister Mandy or her father Ron for over 20 years because of a dispute over a relative's will. Ron has now become seriously ill and needs to go into a nursing home. Carol and Mandy agree, through their respective solicitors, to share the cost of the nursing home equally until such time as their father dies. After only two months a row breaks out between Carol and Mandy and Carol refuses to pay any more towards the nursing home bills. Which of the following statements best represents the legal position between Carol and Mandy?

[A] The agreement between Carol and Mandy is void because, being sisters it is a domestic contract and, therefore, it follows that there was no intention by either party to create a legal relationship.

[B] The agreement between Carol and Mandy is binding on them both because although they are both sisters this is not relevant in this case because the domestic relationship has long since broken down and they did intend to be legally bound.

[C] The agreement between Carol and Mandy is void because although they have not spoken to each other for over 20 years the court will ignore that fact and will hold that the presumption that the parties do not intend to be legally bound has not been rebutted.

[D] The court will ignore the fact that Carol and Mandy are sisters and will hold that the agreement is a commercial one and that, therefore, both parties did intend to create a legal relationship.

22. Carolyn telephones John and offers to sell him £5,000 worth of oriental rugs. John accepts Carolyn's offer and says that he will confirm his acceptance in writing. Carolyn also says that she will confirm their agreement in writing. Carolyn writes to John stating 'Just to confirm the details of our contract: 100 oriental rugs for a total price of £5,000'. On the same day John writes to Carolyn stating 'I promised I would confirm the details of our contract: 150 oriental rugs for a total price of £5,000'. Which of the following situations is correct?

[A] There is an enforceable contract for 100 oriental rugs.
[B] There is an enforceable contract for 150 oriental rugs.
[C] There is an enforceable contract for 125 oriental rugs.
[D] There is no enforceable contract.

23. Which of the following approaches is NOT an effective method to determine the selling price when contractual details are incomplete?

[A] Price to be set by course of dealings between the parties.
[B] A clause stating it to be 'on usual hire purchase terms'.
[C] A clause in a contract providing for arbitration in the event of the parties failing to agree on the price.
[D] Price to be set by referring to the 'market price' on the day of the contract.

24. Jake, aged 17 years, entered into a contract to purchase a car from Arnold, a friend of Jake's mother. The purchase price was £2,400 payable by 24 monthly payments of £100. Jake owes 3 months' payments. Can Arnold successfully sue for the arrears?

[A] Jake will only be liable if the car can be shown to be a 'necessary' taking into consideration his position in life.
[B] Jake will be liable once he becomes 18 years old.
[C] Jake is liable for all the payments.
[D] Jake is not liable for the arrears because a minor cannot be sued in contract.

25. David had always wanted to buy Frank's car. It was a classic car valued at over £10,000. Frank had refused several offers from David including an offer for £14,000. Last week David took Frank to the local public house and Frank became very drunk. David remained sober and offered £11,000 for the car. Frank refused initially but David eventually persuaded him to sign a written contract to sell the car to him. The following day David arrived with a banker's draft for the contract price. Frank is refusing to perform the contract alleging that if he had been sober he would never have signed the contract. Which answer is correct?

[A] Frank is not bound because he lacked the capacity to enter into the contract.
[B] Frank is bound but in these circumstances the court is unlikely to order specific performance.
[C] Frank is bound because drunkenness does not prevent someone understanding the transaction.
[D] The contract is against public policy.

26. Jayling District Council entered into a contract with Cowboy Ltd to build new council offices. The contract contained the usual customary clauses in such contracts, one of which made the council responsible for insuring the work against loss or damage from fire. Cowboy Ltd sub-contracted some of the electrical work to Fred. While smoking during his lunch break, Fred negligently set the building on fire. The new building was destroyed. Fred has just won £20 million on the lottery. The council are suing Fred. Which is the correct answer?

[A] The council can claim from Fred because he owed them a general duty of care.

[B] The council cannot claim from Fred because the council had assumed the risk under the contract with Cowboy Ltd.

[C] Fred was not a party to the contract between the council and Cowboy Ltd and therefore under the rule of privity cannot claim any protection under that contract.

[D] None of the above.

27. Sam lived in a block of flats. The lease was silent in respect of who was responsible for the repair and maintenance of the shared parts. When the landlord refused to repair the lighting and lifts, Sam successfully sued the landlord. The court held that there was an implied duty in the contract to repair and maintain the common parts. Why was the term implied?

[A] The term was implied by fact under the 'officious bystander' test.

[B] The term was implied by fact since it was necessary to give business efficacy to the contract.

[C] The term was implied by law because the court considered it the landlord's duty to maintain the shared parts.

[D] The term was implied in fact because it was reasonable.

28. Bella viewed a flat and agreed to take the tenancy from the day after the present tenants left the flat. Bella signed the tenancy agreement two days before she was due to take up occupation of the flat. The following term was included in the agreement: 'The tenant accepts the flat in good order'. On entering the flat she found the flat was not in good condition. The flat was dirty, the carpets were heavily stained, the cooker was filthy and some of the curtains were missing. Bella wants to end the contract. The landlord is agreeable to putting the flat in order but does not accept the contract is at an end. Which statement is correct? (Ignore any landlord and tenancy legislation.)

[A] There has been a breach of warranty and therefore Bella cannot end the contract.
[B] There has been a breach of condition and therefore Bella can end the contract.
[C] This is an innominate term and in the circumstances Bella could end the contract.
[D] This is an innominate term and in the circumstances it is unlikely that Bella could end the contract.

29. Ben, a keen amateur long-distance cyclist, saw an advertisement in a bicycle shop which read as follows: 'The ABC Mountaineering Bike is the best in its class. It is ideally suited for competition events and is capable of being ridden over the most difficult of terrain. It needs minimum maintenance, spares are cheap and easy to install. Price £1,000.' He entered the shop and discussed the possible purchase of the bike with the retailer. After some discussions as to price Ben purchases the bike for £900. He has been very disappointed with the bike and wants his money back. Ben has discovered that the bike can be purchased elsewhere for £600, it is totally unsuitable for mountaineering and competition events. The spare parts are very expensive and repairs are difficult. Which of the following statements is correct?

[A] The statements in the advertisement are terms of the contract because they have been made by an expert.
[B] Ben saw the advertisement at the time he entered into the contract. Statements made at the time or just before the contract is made are deemed to be terms of the contract.
[C] The advertisement is a misrepresentation. Only statements made during negotiations can be considered terms of a contract.
[D] Advertisements are always an invitation to treat and therefore can never form part of any contract.

30. Modgear, a mail order company, offers for sale a set of six copper saucepans for a price of £66. Their offer states that 'If for any reason you are not entirely satisfied with the saucepans when you have tried them then you can return them at any time within 1 year of receiving them and we will refund your purchase price plus your postage'. Gullible orders the six saucepans. Eleven months later Gullible decides that he is not entirely satisfied with the saucepans and returns them to Modgear. Modgear return the saucepans to Gullible saying that they have examined the saucepans and that there is nothing wrong with them. In an action against Modgear, Gullible will:

[A] Win, because the saucepans are not of satisfactory quality as far as Gullible is concerned.

[B] Win, because it was a condition of the contract that Modgear would take the saucepans back if Gullible was not entirely satisfied with the saucepans.

[C] Lose, because the saucepans are of satisfactory quality.

[D] Lose, because Modgear's promise to take the saucepans back was a mere advertising gimmick and was not incorporated into the contract between Gullible and Modgear.

31. The remedies for an operative negligent misrepresentation are:

[A] Rescission of the contract, and the refusal to perform obligations, and the right to bring an action in the tort of deceit.

[B] Rescission and injunction, plus the right to refuse to perform any contractual obligations.

[C] Rescission or damages, refusal to perform obligations, and damages under the Misrepresentation Act 1967.

[D] Rescission or damages in contract, and the right to refuse to perform obligations, and damages under the Misrepresentation Act 1967.

32. Nelson, an antiques dealer, buys a plate from Matthew for £2 at his local car boot sale. Nelson is almost certain that the plate is a very valuable Dresden piece but does not tell Matthew. Matthew thinks the plate is a worthless trinket but does not tell Nelson this. Matthew's girlfriend, Usha, tells him that she has seen Matthew's plate for sale in Nelson's shop priced at £3,000. What can Matthew do?

[A] Nothing; life is like that.
[B] Rescind the contract and sue for damages for Nelson's fraudulent misrepresentation because Nelson had deceived him.
[C] Declare the contract void for mistake and claim for the return of the plate.
[D] Rescind the contract because of Nelson's innocent misrepresentation.

33. Zoe wants to purchase an art gallery. She goes along to the Pop Deco Art Gallery which is for sale. Peso, the owner of the gallery shows Zoe the books of the company which show an excellent client list and net profits of some £600,000 per year. He honestly forgets to tell her that his best client who generates at least a third of the net profits for the company has moved to New York and that it is very unlikely that he will ever do business with the gallery again. Zoe then buys the gallery for £1.5 million. The contract of sale makes no mention of the profits of the business. Two months later Zoe discovers that the gallery's best customer has moved and that he will never do business with the gallery again. Peso's 'actions' amount to:

[A] A mere representation.
[B] An innocent misrepresentation.
[C] A negligent misrepresentation.
[D] A fraudulent misrepresentation.

34. Which of the following situations gives rise to an operative misrepresentation by the seller?

[A] Fred goes into his local DIY corner shop to buy a drill bit suitable for drilling into masonry. He selects a drill bit which he thinks is suitable for the job; in fact it is not suitable for drilling masonry and the shopkeeper knows that and knows the purpose for which Fred is buying the drill bit but says nothing to Fred. Fred buys the drill bit.

[B] Fred then goes into his local supermarket to buy some hair restorer. He has not used any before but a friend has told him that the best he can buy is Hairiest. He buys the largest can of Hairiest that is available; it is in fact useless.

[C] Fred, who wants a new computer for his business, sees a computer advertised for private sale in his local newspaper. He contacts the seller, Chris, who assures him that the computer is nearly new. Reassured by this Fred buys the computer. In fact the computer is 9 months' old, although Chris has only used the computer a few times since he bought it new. Unknown to Chris the computer's main processor blew up when he last turned the computer off.

[D] Now he has his computer Fred wants to purchase some specialist computer software for his brewing business. He goes along to see an independent software expert who tells him that the best software for his business is BrewSoft. Fred then buys the BrewSoft software for £5,000 from a large independent software house; BrewSoft is not at all suitable for his particular business although it is usually an excellent product for most brewing businesses.

35. At common law an operative mistake renders a contract:

[A] Capable of being rescinded.
[B] Unenforceable.
[C] Voidable.
[D] Void.

36. When establishing an operative unilateral mistake certain factors must be present. Which one of the following statements is correct?

[A] The innocent party must show that he only intended to contract with a real company which he had had previous dealings, the contract was by correspondence and the identity of the real company was essential to the innocent party.

[B] The innocent party must show that the contract was face to face with the rogue, that he only intended to contract with a real person and that the name of the person was important to the innocent party.

[C] The innocent party must show that the contract was either face to face or by correspondence and that the rogue had misrepresented his identity and credit worthiness to the innocent party.

[D] The innocent party must show that the rogue misrepresented his identity to him.

37. Beryl needed glasses to read. She decided to buy a second-hand car from a local car dealer. Included in the purchase price was a 3-year maintenance agreement. The car dealer informed Beryl the maintenance agreement was only valid if certain conditions were met but he did not explain those conditions. Beryl paid cash for the car. Shortly before she was due to collect the car Beryl broke her glasses and the car dealer agreed to deliver the car to her home. On delivery she signed the maintenance agreement without reading it. Beryl's glasses have now been repaired and she has had the opportunity to read the maintenance agreement. Beryl is unhappy about the agreement and would like to cancel the contract, return the car and recover her money. Which of the following answers is correct?

[A] The car dealer has misrepresented to her the contents of the maintenance agreement and therefore she can rescind the contract.

[B] Beryl was unaware of the contents of the contract and therefore she can terminate the contract and recover the money she paid for the car.

[C] Beryl cannot end the contract because she cannot establish either misrepresentation or *non est factum.*

[D] Beryl cannot cancel the contract because once a party has signed a contract they cannot cancel for any reason.

38. Ken, a lonely and insecure person, attends a meeting which had been organized by a time share company. Convinced by the company's representative, Rosemary, that Ken will find love and happiness abroad, he signs an agreement and hands over a cheque for £12,000. The following morning Ken regrets his actions but the company refuse to return his money. For which of the following reasons should Ken claim that the company induced the transaction?

[A] Undue influence.
[B] Duress.
[C] Mistake.
[D] Misrepresentation.

39. Jill and David had been living together for 5 years. David persuaded Jill to use part of her savings to purchase a property. A house was purchased for £95,000. Jill contributed £30,000 and David raised the rest on mortgage. David advised Jill that the house would have to be in his sole name otherwise they would not be able to raise a mortgage. Jill accepted David's advice and agreed to the house being placed in David's sole name. David failed to keep up the mortgage payments because he preferred to spend his money on other things. The bank took possession of the property. The house has just been sold for £80,000. The amount owing on the mortgage was £70,000. Jill claims undue influence and wants the return of all her money. David never intended to deliberately deceive Jill and believed he was purchasing the property to benefit them both. How much of the £30,000 can Jill recover?

[A] Jill can recover all her £30,000.
[B] The net sale proceeds would be split equally between Jill and David.
[C] Jill can recover some or all of the net sale proceeds.
[D] Jill can recover nothing.

40. Peter and Jean lived together in a house owned by Jean. Peter's business began to suffer financial difficulties so he persuaded Jean to use the house as security for his business's overdraft. Peter told Jean the loan was for £20,000. This was untrue. The bank instructed Leg and Co. a firm of solicitors to act for themselves. The bank gave the solicitors instructions that Jean was to receive independent advice before signing the documents. Peter was present at the meeting with the solicitors. The solicitor informed Jean correctly that the security was for an unlimited amount. In the solicitor's presence she signed the documents. Peter's business has now collapsed owing the bank £150,000. The bank is now seeking possession of the house. Jean is claiming the bank is not entitled to possession because of undue influence. Which of the following statements is correct?

[A] The bank cannot enforce the loan because Peter misled Jean in relation to the liability on the house.

[B] The bank has constructive notice of Peter's statement because they were on notice that the loan had no advantage to Jean.

[C] The bank has avoided constructive notice of Peter's undue influence by instructing solicitors to give independent advice to Jean.

[D] The bank is not effected by Peter's misrepresentation because Jean signed the documents and therefore has no defence.

41. Eric pulls up to a car park automatic barrier in his car. A notice clearly visible next to the barrier states the parking charges are £3 per hour. He takes a time stamped ticket from the barrier machine. The barrier opens and he enters the car park and parks his car. Two hours later Eric returns to the car park. In order to leave the car park Eric has to insert his car park ticket in a payment machine. This he does and he pays £6. For which of the following reasons would an exclusion clause be incorporated into the contract between Eric and the car park owner?

[A] The clause was clearly visible at the car park entrance.

[B] The clause was clearly visible on the face of the time stamped ticket.

[C] The clause was clearly visible on a notice in the car park next to the stairs by which Eric left the car park.

[D] None of the circumstances above.

42. The Unfair Terms in Consumer Contracts Regulations 1994 have recently come into force. Which one of the following statements is INCORRECT?

[A] The Regulations only apply to consumer contracts where the contract has not been individually negotiated subject to defined consumer contracts being excluded from the Regulations.
[B] The definition of 'fairness' seems to be similar to the definition of 'reasonableness' under Unfair Contract Terms Act 1977.
[C] The Regulations apply to all terms in the contract.
[D] A consumer under the Regulations is defined as 'a natural person'.

43. The Unfair Contract Terms Act 1977 regulates the enforceability of exclusion clauses. Which one of the following statements is correct?

[A] The test of reasonableness under the Unfair Contract Terms Act 1977 applies to all contracts.
[B] Terms, which attempt to exclude or restrict liability, are void under the Unfair Contract Terms Act 1977.
[C] Exclusion clauses which exclude or restrict liability for personal injury or death are voidable under the Unfair Contract Terms Act 1977.
[D] The Unfair Contract Terms Act 1977 does not apply to a contract where the first party acts in the course of a business and the other party is neither contracting on the first party's standard terms nor is dealing as a consumer and the clause does not attempt to exclude or restrict the implied terms under the Sale of Goods Act 1979.

44. Bess took out a home contents insurance policy with Ince Ltd. The clause defining contents was, *inter alia,* as follows: 'Contents is defined as . . . All property including business equipment, valuables, clothing, personal effects and money in your home owned by any member of your household or for which you are responsible'. Bess's house was burgled when she was at work. The thieves stole, among other things, her brother's camcorder which she had borrowed for the weekend. The insurance company have refused to accept the claim for the camcorder because they argue that Bess was not legally responsible for the camcorder. Which of the following is correct?

[A] The claim is valid because the general interpretation of 'responsible' would apply to this situation.

[B] The claim is not valid because 'responsible' would be restricted to its legal definition and since Bess had not been negligent she is not in breach of her legal duties.

[C] The claim is valid because the clause is unreasonable under s. 11 of the Unfair Contract Terms Act 1977.

[D] The claim is valid because exclusion clauses are interpreted strictly and against the party who is seeking to rely on it.

45. Which of the following statements most accurately outlines the effect of the *contra proferentem* rule?

[A] The person who in fact signs a written contract is deemed to have notice of, and to have accepted, all the terms contained in it, in the absence of misleading information as to their meaning.

[B] The person who seeks to enforce an exclusion clause in a consumer contract must show that it is reasonable.

[C] The words of an exclusion clause will, in the absence of clarity, be construed against the party seeking to rely on it.

[D] The court when construing an exclusion clause presumes it was not intended to work against the principle purpose of the contract.

46. Sheering, a professional footballer, signs a 1-year contract to play for Oldfortress City. A term in his contract states that he must attend for 3 months' training before the first match of the season which is a charity match. Whilst training Sheering is injured in a tackle and as a result he misses the last month's training, the charity match and the first two games of the league season. Which of the following situations best represents the legal position between Sheering and Oldfortress City?

[A] There has been no breach of contract by Sheering and therefore he is not legally liable to Oldfortress City in any way.

[B] By missing the last month's training, the charity match and the first two games of the league season, Sheering has committed a breach of warranty and he therefore has become liable to pay damages to Oldfortress City.

[C] By missing the last month's training, the charity match and the first two games of the league season, Sheering has made a repudiatory breach of contract which entitles Oldfortress City to end their contract with him.

[D] Sheering's contract with Oldfortress City was frustrated when he got injured in the tackle.

47. Which of the following is NOT a definition of the doctrine of frustration of contract?

[A] When that, for which the parties have contracted, has been altered by circumstances which render the contractual 'state of things' essentially different from that which was originally bargained for.

[B] Parties are discharged if an event, for which neither party is responsible, occurs which was not contemplated and it significantly affects that which was originally intended.

[C] The parties who contract that something should be done are discharged if performance becomes impossible because of an event outside of the control of either party.

[D] The parties are discharged where one party knows that that which was contemplated will probably not come to fruition and in the event it does not.

48. Smail and Desmond Ltd agree that Richard should drive one of their restored Lola T70 sports cars in a retro race at Silverstone on 27 August. Richard agreed to this and arrived at Silverstone on 26 August in order to qualify and practice for the actual race on 27 August. For which of the following reasons will the contract be frustrated?

[A] Smail and Desmond Ltd offer a Ford GT 40 in place of the Lola T70 which was damaged in transit on its way to Silverstone as a result of poor loading by Smail and Desmond Ltd.

[B] Following the crash of a Formula 1 car and the death of its driver the governing body of the sport suspends all racing until 1 October.

[C] Due to traffic congestion the event is transferred to Castle Combe.

[D] Smail and Desmond Ltd withdrew the Lola T70 from the retro race because they decided to spend the money that it would have cost to compete in the race on a new car.

49. When do the courts apply the 'blue pencil test' of severance?

[A] Any restraint of trade in a contract is to be severed because it does not promote a legitimate interest.

[B] Any contract containing a provision in restraint of trade is to be deleted because the restraint is unreasonable.

[C] A restraint of trade has to be assessed in order to ensure that it is reasonable from the stand point of society as a whole.

[D] Words will be severed from an agreement in restraint of trade when it is shown that the intention was generally not to impose such a wide restriction.

50. Which of the following agreements is NOT an agreement of 'utmost good faith'?

[A] The fiduciary relationship said to exist between a company director and his company.

[B] A contract of insurance.

[C] The fiduciary relationship between a solicitor and his client.

[D] A preliminary contract between an estate agent and his client.

51. George runs a small engineering company in Oxford. He has entered into an agreement with Lynn to manufacture and supply 'personal electric shock guns'. The manufacture of such guns is against the law. The guns were manufactured and supplied on time. It has now been discovered that such manufacture is both void and illegal at common law. Lynn has since left her home and is reported to be living in Spain. However, she still owes £10,000 to George for the guns as supplied. For which of the following reasons may George be able to recover the guns?

[A] The contract was merely void on the grounds of public policy.
[B] He was unaware the contract was illegal; but Lynn knew that it was, and she fraudulently kept the true position a secret.
[C] The agreement to manufacture was lawful; but illegal by performance.
[D] On a *quantum meruit* to the extent he completed his side of the bargain.

52. In January Jock arranged for Quick Spray to repaint his car. It was agreed that it would be ready for collection by the end of February. At the end of February the car was not ready for collection due to a shortage of qualified staff. In the circumstances Jock reluctantly agreed that he would collect his repainted car at the end of April. At the end of April he discovered from an employee of Quick Spray that the work had not yet been completed. Jock immediately served notice requiring completion of the work by the end of May. If the work is not completed until the middle of June the contract is discharged by which of the following reasons?

[A] Breach.
[B] Agreement.
[C] Frustration.
[D] Performance.

53. Mearl's Performance Parts agree to manufacture a quantity of steel braided brake lines for Henshaw Racing Services. The total agreed contract price is £2,500. Manufacture is to begin on the 1 August, and to be completed by the 27 September. Due to a shortage of steel braid and a strike at Mearl's Performance Parts headquarters, the order is not completed until the 25 October. Mearl's Performance Parts admit to breach of contract but are challenging the amount of damages claimed. The amount of the claim is:

(i)   £5,000 for loss of business during the period of delay from the 27 September to 25 October.
(ii)   £15,000 for the loss of profits on a new contract which was offered to Henshaw Racing Services on the 1 September; but which they could not accept.

What amount of damages will Mearl's Performance Parts have to pay?

[A] £5,000, the normal loss of business profits.
[B] £15,000, as Mearl's Performance Parts should have been aware of the new contract.
[C] No damages because the losses are too remote.
[D] £20,000, all losses are recoverable as it is foreseeable that delay will have a serious consequence.

54. Toby was a manufacturer of various electronic components. Toby gave Herman a licence to make these components. Toby had a reputation of outstanding quality. In the contract between Toby and Herman it was agreed that Herman would pay Toby £50 for every component which was sold and was defective. Two thousand defective components valued at £10 each were sold. Is Toby entitled to damages of £100,000 under the terms of the contract?

[A] Toby is not entitled to damages under the contract because the amount is excessive and unconscionable compared with the actual loss incurred.
[B] If the amount is the same for various events under the contract then the clause is void.
[C] Toby's damages would be assessed on the basis of £10 for each defective component.
[D] The clause is valid because it is impossible to determine the actual loss to Toby in relation to loss of reputation and loss of future sales.

55. Anna is a horticulturist and carries on a business growing and selling exotic plants to retailers. Issac sold Anna a commercial glass house. The contract price included installation of air conditioning and heating in the glass house. Once it was installed Anna began using it for growing highly specialist and delicate plants. Three months later the heating system broke down because of Issac's defective workmanship and Anna lost all the plants in the glass house. The entire stock is valued at £60,000. Anna had entered into a lucrative contract for some of these plants and would have received an additional £20,000. What amount is Anna entitled to?

[A] £80,000 for loss of profit of all the plants in the glass house.
[B] £60,000 for the value of the stock.
[C] Loss of profit and capital expenditure.
[D] Nothing.

56. In the case of discharge by fundamental breach of contract what can an injured party do?

(i) The injured party is entitled to treat the breach as repudiatory and is therefore able to rescind the contract.
(ii) The injured party is entitled to either affirm the contract or reject it.
(iii) If the injured party does nothing then he will be taken to have affirmed the breach.
(iv) The injured party must seek an injunction if he wants to claim damages.

Which of the above statements are correct?

[A] (i) only.
[B] (ii) only.
[C] (i), (ii) and (iii).
[D] (iv) only.

57. What is the basic aim of the award of damages for breach of contract?

[A] To provide that the defaulting party is penalised to prevent the recurrence of the breach.
[B] To guarantee that the defaulting party does not profit from his breach.
[C] To ensure that the injured party receives payment for acts performed.
[D] To ensure that the injured party is in the same position as he would have been in had the contract been performed.

58. Rob, a car enthusiast, enters into a contract with Fantastic Car Builders whereby they agree to build him a hand built car for a fixed price of £300,000. Delivery is to be on 1 October. On that day Fantastic Car Builders deliver the car to Rob who is initially delighted with the car. However, on closer examination Rob discovers that a mirror is missing from the back of the drinks cabinet and that one of the stereo speakers in the back of the car is not working. Rob rejects the car and refuses to pay a penny. Which of the following situations best represents Rob's position?

[A] Rob was wrong in the way he acted. Fantastic Car Builders substantially performed the contract and Rob must pay the full £300,000.
[B] Rob was wrong in the way he acted. He cannot reject the car and he has to pay the £300,000 less a reasonable amount to pay for the mirror and the speaker.
[C] Since the breaches by Fantastic Car Builders are so slight Rob must give them a reasonable time to fix the faults. If the faults are then fixed by Fantastic Car Builders within a reasonable time Rob will then have to pay the full price.
[D] Since the contract is for a fixed price and Fantastic Car Builders have not completed the car by the agreed date Rob has correctly rejected the car and does not have to pay a penny towards it.

59. Steve orders a self-loading automatic handgun from Guns Unlimited for £750. Delivery is to be on 1 December. On 1 October Steve cancels his order because he fears that the government is about to outlaw handguns. Guns Unlimited refuse to accept Steve's cancellation. On 21 October Steve again tries to cancel his order but again Guns Unlimited refuse to accept his cancellation. On 5 November the government introduce a law immediately banning the sale or possession of handguns. On 1 December Guns Unlimited tries to deliver Steve's handgun to him but Steve refuses to accept it. Which of the following situations best represents Guns Unlimited's position?

[A] Guns Unlimited can sue Steve for his anticipatory repudiatory breach of 1 October.

[B] Guns Unlimited can sue Steve for his anticipatory repudiatory breach of 21 October.

[C] Guns Unlimited can sue Steve for his repudiatory breach of 1 December.

[D] Guns Unlimited cannot sue Steve because the delivery of the gun on 1 December would have been illegal.

60. If the issue is one of anticipatory breach of contract when is the injured party entitled to sue?

[A] After a reasonable period of time.

[B] Only from the moment the injured party has satisfied his obligations and the other party says he does not intend to be bound.

[C] Only from the time the other party actually breaches a contractual provision.

[D] From the moment the other party indicates that he does not intend to be bound.

MCT2

[TIME LIMIT: 2½ HOURS]

1. Max offers a reward of £1,000 for information leading to the criminal conviction of Jane, a robber. In which of the following circumstances, if any, is Fred entitled to the reward?

[A] Fred gave the appropriate information to Max but Jane was acquitted.

[B] Unaware of the reward Fred gave the appropriate information to Max which resulted in Jane being convicted of robbery.

[C] Aware of the reward Fred gave the appropriate information to Max which resulted in Jane being convicted of robbery.

[D] None of the above since such rewards are void as being contrary to public policy.

2. Consider the following statements in relation to unilateral offers.

(i) In order to classify an offer as a unilateral offer the offer must be made to the whole world.

(ii) In order to classify an offer as a unilateral offer it must be advertised in such a way that a large number of people become aware of the offer.

(iii) Unilateral offers can never be revoked.

Which, if any, of the above statements are correct?

[A] (i) and (iii).

[B] (ii) and (iii).

[C] None of them.

[D] All of them.

3. On 30 August Simon, a hard-up student, wrote to Wendy offering to sell her his multi-media PC for £1,500. He told her that she could have a week to think the offer over from receipt of the letter; the letter was received by Wendy on 1 October. On 3 October he sold his PC to Carol for £1,600. On 4 October Simon posted a letter to Wendy telling her that he had sold his computer. This letter reached Wendy on 7 October. On 6 October Carol, who is Wendy's best friend, told her that she had bought a multi-media PC from Simon. Wendy was furious at hearing this and immediately wrote to Simon accepting his offer; this letter arrived on 7 October. Which of the following statements is correct?

[A] Simon's offer was revoked on 4 October when Simon posted his letter of revocation.

[B] Simon's offer was revoked on 6 October when Wendy heard from Carol that she had bought Simon's computer.

[C] A contract came into existence on 6 October when Wendy posted her letter of acceptance.

[D] Simon broke his contract with Wendy when he sold his PC to Carol on 3 October.

4. Which of the following is INCORRECT? An offer is always brought to and end by:

[A] The acceptance of the offer.

[B] The expiration of a reasonable time where no time for the ending of the offer has been fixed.

[C] The posting of a counter-offer.

[D] The death of the offeree.

5. Mary is doing her weekly shop for groceries in her local Tesbury's. When does the contract for the sale of 'her' groceries come into existence?

[A] When Mary puts the goods in her shopping trolley.

[B] When Mary hands the goods to the cashier.

[C] When the cashier scans in the price of the goods.

[D] When Mary pays for the goods.

6. At 10.00 hours on 1 May Beef Supplies plc offer to sell 1,000 sides of prime beef to Macburgers plc at a special price of £250 per side; the offer is sent by e-mail. At 12.00 hours on the same day Macburgers plc reply by e-mail to Beef Supplies plc that they'll take all the beef at that price and anymore they've got at that price. Macburgers plc's e-mail is received by Beef Supplies plc at 12.30 hours that day but because of the illness of a salesman it is not read until 09.00 hours the following day. At 13.00 hours on 1 May Beef Supplies plc sold the 1,000 sides of beef to Wimpburgers plc for £260 per side. At 13.30 hours on 1 May Beef Supplies plc e-mailed Macburgers plc to say that their offer was withdrawn; this e-mail was read at 14.30 hours by an authorised employee. Which of the following statements is a court most likely to say represents the position between Beef Supplies plc and Macburgers plc?

[A] Since the postal rules apply to e-mails a contract between Beef Supplies plc and Macburgers plc for the 1,000 sides of beef came into existence at 12.00 hours on 1 May.

[B] The e-mail sent at 12.00 hours was a counter offer and therefore destroyed Beef Supplies plc's original offer.

[C] Since Macburgers plc's e-mail accepting the offer was not read until 09.00 hours on 2 May Beef Supplies plc effectively withdrew their offer at 14.30 hours on 1 May when their e-mail was read by an authorised employee of Macburgers plc.

[D] Macburgers plc's acceptance will be treated as having been received by Beef Supplies plc when it was received by them at 12.30 hours on 1 May even though it was not seen by any member of their staff until the following day.

7. Peter advertises his car for sale for £500. Sally, who is anxious to buy a cheap car, approaches Peter and tells him that she is very interested in buying his car but that she needs to borrow some money from her parents in order to be able to buy the car. Peter tells Sally that there are lots of people interested in his car and that if she wants him to hold on to it for her she must give him £50 now to keep his offer open to her for 14 days. Sally agrees to this and gives £50 to Peter. Ten days later Sally borrows £500 from her parents and she approaches Peter. Which of the following actions can Sally now take?

[A] Accept Peter's offer only if he has not already sold the car to someone else.

[B] Accept Peter's offer even if he has already sold the car to someone else and even though she knows it has been sold before she tries to accept Peter's offer.

[C] Accept Peter's offer even if he has already sold the car to someone else if she does not know that it has already been sold.

[D] Sue Peter for fraudulent misrepresentation if he has already sold the car to someone else.

8. For the past 5 years Foxclean have had a contract to clean Rabbit Ltd's office building. When the contract was due for renewal Rabbit Ltd decided to put it out to tender. They wrote to 8 firms, including Foxclean, inviting them to submit a tender for the cleaning contract. The letter of invitation stipulated that the tender must include full details of price and services proposed, must be in a sealed envelope, and must reach Rabbit Ltd's offices no later than 3 p.m. on 25 April. Foxclean gave their tender direct to Rabbit Ltd's receptionist at 2 p.m. on 25 April. The receptionist did not realise its importance and failed to pass on the tender for 3 days to the relevant department. Rabbit Ltd assumed the tender had arrived late and ignored it. They awarded the tender to one of the other companies who had submitted a tender. Foxclean Ltd are horrified because they were favourites to win the contract. Rabbit Ltd have now discovered the error but argue that the matter is regrettable and the contract has already been awarded to someone else. Can Foxclean claim damages from Rabbit Ltd?

[A] Yes, Rabbit Ltd are liable to the extent that they should have considered the bid because Foxclean Ltd had complied with all the conditions of the request.

[B] No, letters requesting such tenders are invitations to treat and therefore Rabbit Ltd are not liable.

[C] Yes, letters requesting tenders are offers and therefore Rabbit Ltd are liable.

[D] No, Rabbit Ltd are not liable because they have already offered the contract to somcone clse.

9. Consider the following statements. An enforceable contract must:

(i)   Show that acceptance has been communicated to the offeror.
(ii) Show that the parties intended to create legal relations.
(iii) Show that both parties furnished consideration.

Which, if any, of the above statements are correct?

[A] (ii) and (iii).
[B] All of them.
[C] (ii) only.
[D] (iii) only.

10. Nuneaton University placed an advertisement in Oil Suppliers Monthly inviting tenders to supply the university with fuel oil for its central heating. Slick Oil Ltd submitted a tender by which it agreed to supply 'such quantities of fuel oil as may be required from 1 October to 30 August at the market price obtaining at the time of order less 5%'. Nuneaton University accepted this tender. The university placed an order in November which Slick Oil Ltd supplied in accordance with the terms of the agreement. Because of the extremely mild weather the second order was not placed until March. Slick Oil Ltd considers that the university has not honoured the spirit of the agreement by only placing two orders in the winter months and therefore refuses to supply the oil requested in the second order. Which of the following statements is correct?

[A]   Slick Oil Ltd is in breach of the contract to supply the oil throughout the year which came into existence when Nuneaton University accepted Slick Oil Ltd's tender.

[B]   Slick Oil Ltd is not in breach of the March contract because Nuneaton University's March order only amounted to an offer to Slick Oil Ltd which Slick Oil Ltd was free to either accept or reject.

[C]   Slick Oil Ltd is in breach of the contract to supply the oil ordered in March although it can tell Nuneaton University that it will supply no further oil in the future.

[D]   Slick Oil Ltd is in breach of the contract to supply the oil ordered in March and cannot tell Nuneaton University that it will supply no further oil in the future since it is bound to honour its obligation to supply oil as and when required.

11. In which of the following circumstances is executed consideration present?

[A]   A contract to deliver goods in a week's time, the goods to be paid for 'cash on delivery'.

[B]   Colin buys a TV set which he pays for in two instalments. The first payment he paid on signing the contract the second he is to pay in a month's time.

[C]   Ingrid's friendly neighbour Tony washes her car for her. Afterwards Ingrid gives Tony £2 to buy a pint.

[D]   Martin has agreed to sell his spare squash racket to Rob. Martin was supposed to give Rob the racket last week but forgot to do so.

12. Which of the following did the plaintiff ONLY have to establish in *Shanklin Pier Ltd* v *Detel Products Ltd* [1951] 2 KB 854?

[A] The existence of a main contract.
[B] That in addition to the main contract (the sale of paint), there was a collateral contract.
[C] That the contractors were agents for the defendants.
[D] That the warranty stood independent from the main contract.

13. Ted agrees to sell 100 tons of barley to Freda for £5,000 and 100 tons of wheat to her for £6,000. As part of the agreement Ted agrees to deliver the wheat and barley to Freda or her nominee if she sells the wheat or barley on. The agreed date of delivery is 29 February. Freda sells the barley to Gretta for £5,500 and instructs Ted to deliver the barley to Gretta. Gretta agrees to pay Ted £200 if he delivers the barley to her on 29 February. Freda asks Ted to deliver 50 tons of the wheat to her on 10 February and tells him that if he does so she will pay him an extra £100; Ted agrees to make the delivery on 10 February. Ted has now completed all the deliveries but Freda and Gretta are refusing to pay him; they both claim that he is not entitled to any money beyond that which Freda agreed to pay him in the original contract. Which of the following statements is correct?

[A] Ted is entitled to both the £200 and the £100.
[B] Ted is only entitled to the £200.
[C] Ted is only entitled to the £100.
[D] Ted is not entitled to either the £200 or the £100.

14. Which of the following cases is authority for the principle that payment of a smaller sum cannot be satisfaction for a larger debt unless there is accord and satisfaction?

[A] *Central London Property Trust* v *High Trees House* [1947] KB 130.
[B] *Foakes* v *Beer* (1884) 9 App Cas 605.
[C] *Welby* v *Drake* (1825) 1 C & P 557.
[D] *Combe* v *Combe* [1951] 2 KB 215.

15. In *Central London Property Trust Ltd* v *High Trees House Ltd* [1947] KB 130, the landlord of a block of flats sued the tenants for the rent that he had forgone in the last two quarters of 1945. Which of the following statements is correct?

[A] The court held that the landlord could recover the rent for the last two quarters but that he was estopped from claiming the lost rent for the previous quarters.

[B] The court held that the landlord could recover the rent for the last two quarters and the lost rent from the previous quarters since the tenants had furnished no fresh consideration for the landlord's promise to forgo the rent.

[C] The court held that the landlord could recover the rent for the last two quarters.

[D] The court held that the landlord was estopped from recovering any monies.

16. Which of the following is the most accurate description of a condition precedent?

[A] It is a major term of a contract by which the parties agree during contractual negotiations how much compensation should be payable by way of damages should a breach of contract occur.

[B] It is a major contractual term which if not performed by one party will absolve the other party from having to perform his side of the contract.

[C] It is a major contractual term introduced when the contract is formed, which provides for discharge on the occurrence of a specified event.

[D] It is a major contractual term breach of which will automatically discharge the contract.

17. Which of the following is NOT an exception to the doctrine of privity of contract?

[A] Where a party to the contract sues upon the contract for specific performance for the benefit of a third party.

[B] Where a contract is made only for the benefit of a third party and if the contract is broken the promisee can generally sue upon it and claim damages for the benefit of the third party.

[C] Damages can be recovered by a trustee for the benefit of the beneficiary provided there was an intention to create a trust.

[D] Where a contract is made between an agent and a third party which binds the agent's principal.

18. Norma specialises in providing top class catering for wedding receptions in the home. She has a reputation for reliability and quality. Norma entered into a contract with Ricky to provide the catering and wine for his daughter's wedding reception. She purchased a large consignment of wine from Jenkins, a wine wholesaler. It was agreed that Norma would take delivery of the wine the day before the reception. On the day of delivery Jenkins refused to deliver the wine unless Norma paid a higher price. Norma reluctantly paid the increase in price. At such short notice there was no possibility of finding another supplier and she had to consider her reputation. Norma would like to recover the difference in price between the amount she actually paid and the amount which was originally agreed. Which is correct?

[A] Norma cannot recover the amount because she agreed to the increase.

[B] Norma can recover the amount because it amounts to duress.

[C] Norma cannot recover the extra payment because by ensuring the wine was delivered on time Jenkins provided fresh consideration.

[D] Norma can recover the extra payment because, although Jenkins may be able to show that he furnished fresh consideration, she agreed under economic duress.

19. Which of the following situations will NOT result in a valid contract?

[A] Vic agrees to audit Jeanette's accounts for a price to be agreed between themselves at a later date but failing such agreement by arbitration conducted by the ACCA. They have conducted their business this way for several years and have only had to resort to arbitration on two previous occasions.

[B] An arbitration clause in a contract between Barry and Hank provides for arbitration of any dispute in London and of any other dispute in New York.

[C] Denise agrees to sell her car to Frank on the usual hire purchase terms. Both Denise and Frank are private individuals who have never dealt with each other before.

[D] George agrees to sell 1,000 tons of wheat to Harriet for £50 per ton but they cannot agree all the fine detail of the transaction. They therefore agree to make an interim agreement until they agree a permanent solution to the fine detail.

20. A contract which lacks certainty is:

[A] Void.
[B] Voidable.
[C] Repudiated.
[D] Unenforceable.

21. Morse and Levis wish to enter into an agreement for the sale and purchase of antique furniture. However, they intend that the agreement will not be legally enforceable. In which of the following ways may they achieve this desire?

[A] By making their agreement under seal.
[B] By including in their agreement a clause to the effect that their agreement will not be legally enforceable.
[C] By not recording their agreement in writing.
[D] By not having their agreement witnessed.

22. Robert has promised to take Mandy his girlfriend to Royal Ascot in return for her making a small contribution to the petrol cost. Mandy is now unsure whether they have entered into legal relations or not. For which of the following reasons will the court imply the intention to enter into legal relations?

[A] The agreement is part of a matrimonial separation agreement in writing.
[B] The agreement is a social domestic agreement.
[C] The agreement is 'subject' to contract.
[D] The agreement is based on warmth and good intention.

23. Four months ago Jim, aged 17, purchased a motorbike from Motors Ltd. Jim bought the motorbike for riding for pleasure at weekends. His school was only a 100 metres away from home and he had a 2 minute walk to the supermarket where he worked part-time. Jim purchased the motorbike on Motors Ltd standard terms of credit. The purchase price was £1,800 repayable over 3 years. Jim's mother acted as guarantor of the loan. A month ago he crashed the motorbike. The accident was not insured under his insurance policy. Soon afterwards Jim lost his job and was unable to make any further payments under the loan. Motors Ltd then demanded that Jim's mother pay the balance due under the guarantee. Jim's mother refused to pay because she claimed that Jim is a minor and therefore did not have the capacity to make a contract. Which is the correct answer?

[A] The guarantee is enforceable because the principal contract is for necessaries and because transport would be considered a necessary.
[B] A guarantor is never liable where the principal contract is with a minor.
[C] A guarantee is not unenforceable against the guarantor merely because the principal obligation was unenforceable against the debtor because he was a minor when he incurred it.
[D] A guarantor is not liable under the guarantee where the main contract was made by a minor for goods which were not necessary.

24. Terms may be implied into a contract by:

(i)   The court, to replace an express term which is not 'usual'.
(ii) Trade practice and usage.
(iii) The court to provide for events not originally contemplated.
(iv) The court to establish important provisions which the parties had overlooked, but which they would have included in the contract if they had thought about it.

Which of the above statements, if any, are correct?

[A]   (ii) and (iv).
[B]   (i) only.
[C]   (iii) only.
[D]   None of the above.

25. Under a 5-year contract Josie obtained a marketing franchise for Smelly Perfumes. It was a condition of the contract that she must visit certain named retailers once a month. Josie found visiting once a month too frequent and made the visits every 6 weeks instead. Smelly Perfumes wanted to repudiate the contract in order to reorganise its business. When Smelly Perfume discovered the visits were 6 weekly it repudiated the contract for Josie's breach. At the time of the repudiation the contract had 2 years to run. Which of the following statements is correct?

[A]   Smelly Perfumes can repudiate the contract because Josie is in breach of a term in the contract.
[B]   Since the contract stipulates that a breach of this term amounts to a breach of condition, Smelly Perfumes can repudiate since a breach of condition entitles the innocent party to repudiate.
[C]   Smelly Perfumes cannot repudiate the contract because the breach is minor and therefore does not justify repudiation.
[D]   Smelly Perfumes can repudiate and claim damages from Josie for being in breach of a term in the contract.

26. A term can be implied into a contract for which of the following reasons?

[A] By custom.
[B] By statute.
[C] By law.
[D] All of the above.

27. Wim is an amateur disc jockey. He agreed to work last Wednesday night at the Anchorage Club. The club agreed to provide Wim with all the necessary equipment for his show, including a selection of 70 long-playing records. The club also agreed to pay Wim £100 for his performance on Wednesday. When Wim arrived he found that there were only 20 long-playing records available. Wim then told the manager that he would not perform and left. The club then contacted Dino and paid him £200 for his Wednesday appearance in place of Wim. Consider the following:

(i) The club, has committed a breach of condition by supplying only 20 long-playing records.
(ii) The club, by supplying only 20 long-playing records, has committed neither a breach of condition nor warranty but an 'innominate term'.
(iii) The club has committed an anticipatory breach of contract.
(iv) Wim is in breach of contract by leaving and refusing to perform the contract.

Which of the above answers, if any, are most accurate?

[A] (i) only.
[B] (ii) only.
[C] (iii) and (iv).
[D] (ii) and (iv).

28. Whilst Ross was selling his speed boat to Mary, he said 'the boat is a sound old tub but I would advise you to have her surveyed just in case'. If Mary buys the boat without a survey what is Ross's statement most LIKELY to constitute?

[A]   A mere 'puff'.
[B]   A warranty.
[C]   A 'mere' representation.
[D]   A term.

29. When a contract is in writing there is a presumption that neither party can rely on extrinsic evidence to vary the written contractual document. To which of the following situations would the parole evidence rule apply?

[A]   Where the written agreement is not the whole agreement.
[B]   When the court is attempting to establish the validity of the contract.
[C]   Where the court was only trying to identify the implied terms of the contract.
[D]   None of the above.

30. In June 1995 Abraham entered into a contract with Overseas Wines whereby Overseas Wines were exclusively to supply Abraham with exotic wines. The contract prevented Abraham from obtaining supplies from elsewhere for 3 years. At the end of 1995 the UK market suffered a slump in the sales of exotic wines. Overseas Wines had similar contracts with other retailers in the UK. Overseas Wines decided to discount the wine to certain retailers. They discounted the wine to two outlets in Abraham's town but he was excluded from the scheme. Abraham found another supplier of exotic wine in order to compete. Overseas Wines brought an action against Abraham for breach of contract. Abraham argued that the agreement was subject to an implied obligation not to discriminate against him in favour of competing local retailers and that Overseas Wines by offering to discount the wine to some retailers but not himself was in breach of that term. Which answer is correct?

[A]   Such a term would be implied because it gives business efficacy to the contract.
[B]   The term would be implied because there is a compelling and essential reason for it to be included.
[C]   The term would be implied because it was fair and reasonable in the circumstances to do so.
[D]   None of the above.

31.   Which one of the following statements can constitute a misrepresentation?

[A]   A statement of law.
[B]   A statement of opinion.
[C]   A statement of intention.
[D]   A statement of fact.

32. Goddard offers to sell a case of his fine old port from his cellar to Denning for £850. Denning knows that Goddard only drinks the finest old vintage port so he writes to Goddard accepting his offer to sell a case of his fine old vintage port for £850. When the port is delivered to Denning he discovers that the port is not vintage port. Denning's best remedy will be:

[A] To rescind the contract and sue for the return of his £850 on the basis that Goddard made a fraudulent misrepresentation by not correcting his misunderstanding of what really was on offer.

[B] To rescind the contract and sue for damages under s. 2 of the Misrepresentation Act 1967 (negligent misrepresentation).

[C] To sue for the return of his £850 since the contract is void for mistake.

[D] None – *caveat emptor*.

33. Steve wants to purchase a restaurant. He goes along to the Chic Restaurant which is for sale. Emma, the owner of the restaurant, shows Steve the books of the company which show an excellent client list and net profits of some £400,000 per year for the previous 2 years. Unknown to Emma, but easily discoverable by her had she bothered to check, was a mistake in the company's books which was due to a simple arithmetical mistake by her accountant. Emma offers to let Steve take the books away for checking but he says that that will not be necessary as he trusts her. Steve then buys the restaurant for £600,000. The contract of sale makes no mention of the profits of the business. Seven months later Steve's accountant points out to him the mistake in the restaurant's books and that the net profit for the previous two years was only £200,000 per year. Which of the following is a remedy for Steve?

[A] None since there was no breach of a term of the contract.

[B] None since Steve should have checked the profits of the business before he bought it.

[C] Rescission of the contract and damages on the grounds of misrepresentation by Emma.

[D] Rescission of the contract and an indemnity on the grounds of misrepresentation by Emma.

34. Joe hired a room to view the Potting Hill Carnival which is held every year. He hired the room for 1 day only, 28 August. Unbeknown to both Joe and the landlord the carnival had already been cancelled for security reasons. Joe is refusing to pay the landlord for the hire of the room. Which of the following statements is correct?

[A] The contract is frustrated.
[B] The contract is void for mistake.
[C] The contract is enforceable.
[D] None of the above.

35. James was a director of a company on a 5-year fixed term contract. The company wished to terminate his contract. Negotiations between James and the company took place and it was agreed that his contract would be severed. Under the terms of the severance James was paid £75,000. Unbeknown to both parties at the time of the agreement James had broken some terms of his contract which would have enabled the company to sever the contract without making any payments to James. The company has discovered its mistake and wants the payment returned. Can the company recover the £75,000?

[A] Yes, the severance contract is void for mistake.
[B] Yes, the severance contract is voidable for mistake.
[C] Yes, the severance contract is valid.
[D] Yes, the severance contract is frustrated.

36. What equitable relief will be UNAVAILABLE for a contract entered into under a mutual mistake?

[A] Compromise.
[B] Injunction.
[C] Actual refusal by the court to grant a decree of specific performance.
[D] Any written documents may be rectified.

37. Alex sells a large painting to Betty for £3,000. Alex and Betty both believed it to be by a little known Lutonian artist. One month later Betty discovers it is worth £450,000 because the painting is, in fact, by Monet. Betty agrees to sell it to a London dealer for £450,000. Consider the following remedies:

(i) The assistance of equity can be invoked and rescission on the grounds of common mistake.

(ii) The contract may be claimed to be void for mistake as to quality.

(iii) Misrepresentation can be claimed.

(iv) An injunction to prevent the sale can be asked for.

Which IF ANY of the above remedies are LIKELY to be available to Alex?

[A] (i) only.
[B] (ii) only.
[C] (iii) and (iv).
[D] None of the above.

38. Tom started attending evening classes in religion. He had tremendous respect for the lecturer, Natasha. They became close friends. They saw each other most days of the week. Tom started attending Natasha's church. Natasha persuaded Tom to donate £20,000 to the 'Church of Sanctity of Spiritual Well Being'. A month later Natasha started seeing Edward from the class and lost interest in Tom. Tom feels betrayed and bitter. He wants his £20,000 returned. Which of the following is correct?

[A] Tom made a gift of his own free will and therefore the money is not returnable.
[B] Natasha has exerted duress on Tom by persuading him to donate moneys to the church and therefore the money is returnable.
[C] There is no presumption of undue influence but this could be established if Tom can show Natasha used her position to dominate his will. Only then will the money be returnable.
[D] There is a presumption of undue influence because Natasha is a lecturer and Tom is a student and therefore the money is returnable.

39. A lift used in a university's law department was regularly used to carry equipment, books and stationery. Whilst carrying a large load of books, stationery and expensive office equipment the lift caught fire and everything within it was destroyed. The insurance policy contained an exclusion clause which exempted the insurers from liability for damages caused 'whilst the lift is carrying more than four persons'. The contents of the lift on this occasion was far more than the weight of four people. The insurers are refusing to pay out because the weight in the lift was in excess of the maximum weight allowable. Does the clause exclude liability?

[A] No; the *contra preferentum* rule will apply. Persons are not the same as books, stationery or office equipment, therefore the exemption clause does not apply.

[B] Yes; a reasonable person would interpret the clause as excluding liability in respect of the carriage of excessive loads and weights rather than only relating to people. The clause is therefore valid.

[C] Yes; exemption clauses are interpreted in the same way as other terms in a contract. Due consideration would be given to the intention of the parties. The insurers are excluding weight and therefore the clause is valid.

[D] Yes; the *contra preferentum* rule is not applicable because it only applies to consumer contracts.

40. Alpha Ltd, whose main business is the production of first-class software, purchased computer hardware and software from DEF Ltd. The contract was on DEF Ltd's usual written terms subject to a few minor amendments. The contract contained an exclusion clause which limited DEF Ltd's liability to £10,000. This amount was far below the loss that Alpha Ltd had suffered. Which of the following statements is correct?

[A] The Unfair Contract Terms Act 1977 does not apply to this contract because Alpha Ltd is not a consumer.

[B] The Unfair Contract Terms Act 1977 does not apply to this contract because this is not a consumer contract and the contract has been individually negotiated.

[C] The Unfair Contract Terms Act 1977 will apply to this contract because Alpha Ltd will be deemed to be acting as a consumer within the meaning of *R & B Customs Brokers Co. Ltd* v *United Dominions Trust Ltd* [1988] 1 WLR 321.

[D] The Unfair Contract Terms Act 1977 will apply to this contract because it is made between two businesses and one party is contracting on the other's standard written terms.

41. Joe, a maker of office furniture, sold a large oak desk and four chairs to Probe Ltd for use in their offices. The standard written contract, which Probe Ltd had seen before in several previous transactions, contained the following clause: 'If the buyer is not dealing as a consumer then we are not liable for any defects or faults in workmanship or breach of any implied statutory terms in respect of the goods supplied, howsoever caused, including negligence, unless notification is made of any such defaults within 3 days of purchase. In such circumstances a full refund will be offered.' A week after the desk and chairs arrived Probe Ltd had an office reorganisation and the desk which cost £1,000 had to be moved. When it was moved, two of the legs snapped. It was then discovered that the desk was only partially made of oak and the legs had been negligently fitted to the desk. Which one of the following statements is INCORRECT?

[A] The clause is not automatically void but is subject to the test of reasonableness under s. 11 of the Unfair Contract Terms Act 1977 because although this is a standard written contract Probe Ltd is not dealing as a consumer.

[B] At common law the clause may well be sufficient to protect Joe since it expressly mentions negligence and is clear in its effect.

[C] At common law the clause is incorporated because Probe Ltd has seen the clause before because of previous dealings.

[D] The clause is reasonable because the parties have a similar strength of bargaining power and Probe Ltd had notice of the clause.

42. Daisy Farm purchased an agricultural machine from Agro Ltd on the latter's standard written terms. Because of a defect in the installation the machine broke down and Daisy Farm suffered a loss of £70,000. Agro Ltd admits liability, but seeks to rely on an exemption clause which limits their liability to £9,000 being the equivalent cost of replacement of the machine. Agro Ltd has product liability of £1 million and is the only importer of the machine into England. Daisy Farm will have difficulty covering the loss. The farm managers saw a copy of the contract before signing it. Is the clause reasonable under s. 11 of the Unfair Contract Terms Act 1977?

[A]   Yes. The clause is reasonable because the contract is between two businesses. The companies are therefore of equal bargaining power. Daisy Farm had knowledge of the clause before signing the contract and once signed a party is bound.

[B]   It is irrelevant as to whether the clause is reasonable under the Unfair Contract Terms Act 1977 because the correct test is one of fairness under the Unfair Terms in Consumer Contracts Regulations 1994.

[C]   No. The clause is not reasonable. There is no equality of bargaining power. Agro Ltd has more than sufficient product liability to meet the claims and Daisy Farm will experience serious financial difficulties.

[D]   None of the above.

43. Which of the following is the *reason* why the decision in *Thompson* v *London Midland and Scottish Rly* [1930] 1 KB 41 could not be repeated today?

[A]   Constructive notice of an exclusion clause has been abolished by current legislation.

[B]   A plaintiff in Mrs Thompson's position could rely on the doctrine of *non est factum.*

[C]   The Unfair Contract Terms Act 1977 makes it unlawful to include a provision in a contract which attempts to exclude liability for death and personal injury.

[D]   Terms that exclude liability for death or personal injury due to negligence in contracts of the type that occurred in *Thompson* v *London Midland and Scottish Rly* are now void under the provisions of the Unfair Contract Terms Act 1977.

44. Pear agrees to transport Apple's perishable goods from Luton to Paris by road on 22 November for a special discount rate of £2,000 although this will only leave Pear with £200 profit for the trip. The reason that Pear is able to offer this special price is that he has a special deal with Eurotunnel who have undercut the ferry prices by a significant margin. Just before Pear is to load Apple's goods there is a fire in the tunnel the consequence of which is that the tunnel is unlikely to be able to take goods lorries for at least 4 weeks. Although Pear could take Apple's goods by sea this would cost him an extra £300 which would mean that he would make a £100 loss on his deal with Apple; Pear therefore refuses to transport Apple's goods to Paris. Which of the following statements would be a remedy for Apple?

[A]   None, because the closure of the tunnel, being the expected route of transport by Pear, would result in the contract being frustrated.

[B]   None, because Pear would now make a loss of £100 instead of a profit of £200. This would mean that there had been a significant change in the nature of the contract with the result that the contract would be frustrated.

[C]   Pear's refusal to carry Apple's goods would be a repudiatory breach of contract which Apple could accept, find another carrier, and claim from Pear the difference in cost between the new carrier's price and the price that Pear had agreed with Apple.

[D]   Pear's refusal to carry Apple's goods would be a repudiatory breach of contract which Apple could accept, find another carrier, and claim from Pear the difference in cost between the new carrier's price and the market price that Pear would have charged Apple if the special deal had not been available from Eurotunnel.

45. Consider the following statements:

(i)   A frustrating event brings the contract to an end.
(ii)   The breach of a condition in a contract brings the contract to an end.

Which of the above statements are correct?

[A]   (i) only.
[B]   (ii) only.
[C]   Both of them.
[D]   Neither of them.

46. In which of the following situations would a contract be discharged by frustration?

[A]   Mavis booked a hotel room for 2 nights to visit the sights of London and attend a concert. The concert was cancelled.
[B]   Neil entered into a contract to deliver wheat from Canada to Tim in England by 3 March 1996. The ship carrying the wheat did not leave port until 1 March and then ran aground because of a storm. As of June 1996 the ship is still under repair and is unlikely to be ready to sail until August 1996.
[C]   Peter hired a room to look at a street carnival. The carnival was cancelled at the last minute due to fears for crowd safety.
[D]   Quentin a builder entered into a contract to build an extension for Simon. Quentin expected the work to last 3 months. Due to a shortage of materials the extension took 12 months to complete.

47. What is the purpose of an injunction?

[A]   The enforcement of a negative restraint in a contract.
[B]   To compel the performance of a contractual term which is not specifically enforceable.
[C]   To ensure the timely compliance and performance.
[D]   To restrain an employee from breaking his obligation to work when his contract contained a negative provision.

48. What is a contract in restraint of trade?

[A] Void.
[B] Voidable.
[C] Void except insofar as reasonable.
[D] Valid.

49. The courts will declare a clause in a contract of employment *prima facie* in restraint of trade and therefore *void* where it is intended to protect:

[A] An employer's good will from being poached by ex-employees.
[B] An employer from the competition of an ex-employee.
[C] An employer's trade secrets from disclosure.
[D] An employer's patent and trade marks.

50. Boilers Ltd contracted with Andrews Ltd to build a boiler for Andrews Ltd. It was agreed as part of the terms that payment for the boiler would not be made until the boiler was completed and installed at Andrew Ltd's factory. The boiler took 6 months to complete. The boiler arrived on 16 May. On 18 May, before the boiler was installed, there was a terrible storm and the factory and the boiler were destroyed. Boilers Ltd are demanding payment and Andrews Ltd are claiming the contract is frustrated. Which of the following answers is correct?

[A] The contract was not frustrated because the work under the contract has nearly been completed and therefore Boilers Ltd is entitled to payment on a *quantum merit* basis.
[B] The contract is frustrated but under the Law Reform (Frustrated Contracts) Act 1943 the loss will be shared equally between the parties.
[C] The contract is frustrated but under the Law Reform (Frustrated Contracts) Act 1943 Andrews Ltd will have to reimburse Boilers Ltd's costs of building the boiler.
[D] Under the common law the contract is frustrated and Boilers Ltd can recover nothing from Andrews Ltd.

51. Arnold agrees to buy a new SuperMan Rotavator from Zed, who runs a garden centre, for £1,500 to rotavate his large allotment. Arnold is very fortunate to be able to buy a SuperMan Rotavator at the list price because they are in very short supply. Later Arnold finds that a friend of his at the pub has a nearly new SuperMan Rotavator for sale at a price of £1,100; Arnold agrees to buy it and takes delivery of it the following day. He then informs Zed that he is cancelling his order for the SuperMan Rotavator. Zed is particularly annoyed by this since Arnold has renegued on deals with him before. In a fit of pique Zed sells the SuperMan Rotavator to the first person who comes into his garden centre for £1,200. If fact if Zed had waited a day or two he could have got £200 over the list price for his SuperMan Rotavator. In an action by Zed against Arnold for breach of contract which of the following by way of damages will he recover from Arnold:

[A]   Nothing.
[B]   £100.
[C]   £300.
[D]   £200.

52. Joe was having his shop refitted by Boggins. The written contract stated that the work must be finished by 1 June otherwise for every week the work is not completed Boggins must pay Joe £10,000. Because of a skilled labour shortage Boggins was 4 weeks late in finishing the work. Before the refit Joe was making a profit of £6,000 per week. During the refit the profits dropped to £3,000. Is Joe entitled to £40,000 from Boggins?

[A]   Yes. Joe is entitled to payment because Boggins was aware of the clause before entering into the contract.
[B]   Yes. Boggins must pay because the sum relates to one stipulation and therefore it is a liquidated damage clause.
[C]   No. Boggins does not have to pay the £40,000 because under the Unfair Terms in Consumer Contracts Regulations 1994 the clause would be considered unfair.
[D]   No. Boggins does not have to pay the £40,000 because the clause would be considered to be excessive.

53. What is a liquidated damages clause?

[A] A penalty clause in a contract payable on demand.
[B] A penalty clause activated by the injured party.
[C] A pre-estimate of the genuine damages payable following breach.
[D] An onerous clause in a contract which will not be enforced.

54. Tom made a contract with Bill to build a house. Tom loves high ceilings and therefore stipulated in the contract that the height of the rooms were to be 3 metres. Unfortunately Bill forgot to mention this requirement to his subcontractors who built the rooms at the usual height of 2.3 metres. Tom is now suing Bill for the price of reconstructing the house at the required height. The breach of contract has not reduced the value of the property. What can Tom recover?

[A] Only loss of amenity and pleasure because there is no loss of value.
[B] Sufficient damages to cover the cost of reconstruction.
[C] Only nominal damages because there is no loss of value.
[D] Loss of amenity and pleasure and the cost of reconstruction.

55. In which of the following circumstances is it UNLIKELY that a decree of specific performance will be granted?

[A] When a contract is for the sale of goods where the goods are made to measure shoes.
[B] When a contract is made by deed for the disposition of land by gift.
[C] When the contract is to pay money to a third party.
[D] When the contract is for the sale of land.

56. Sandra, a poultry farmer, has 2,000 tons of spare chicken feed. She agrees to sell it to her neighbour, Paul, to help him out of a fix caused by his supplier letting him down. It now turns out that Sandra needs the 2,000 tons because she has miscalculated her requirements and that in any case Paul does not now require the 2,000 tons because his supplier has just been able to deliver his order. Sandra and Paul therefore decide to call their deal off. For which of the following reasons has their original contract been discharged?

[A]   Accord and satisfaction.
[B]   Rescission.
[C]   Variation.
[D]   Waiver.

57. *Cutter* v *Powell* (1795) 6 Term Rep 320 states that for a contract to be discharged by performance it must be total and exact. Which of the following is NOT an exception to the harsh rule?

[A]   Substantial performance.
[B]   Severable contracts.
[C]   Acceptance of partial performance.
[D]   Specific performance.

58. Nici agrees to buy a television set from Balti, an electrical retailer. It is agreed that delivery will take place on 1 November. On 1 October Nici informs Balti that as she has just been given a TV set by her aunt and therefore she is cancelling her order. Which of the following best represents Balti's position?

[A]   Balti can sue Nici immediately.
[B]   Balti will have to wait until 1 November when the contract was due for performance before they can sue Nici.
[C]   Balti will first have to tender performance by attempting to deliver the TV set before they can sue Nici.
[D]   Balti will have to write to Nici and give her a reasonable time to perform her side of the contract.

59. Christopher, a university research assistant, signed a contract in July 1997 with Speedy Travel agreeing to carry documents to Singapore. In September 1997 Christopher was offered a more profitable position with another firm, and he wrote to Speedy Travel purporting to cancel the contract with them. Which statement is INCORRECT in relation to Speedy Travel's legal position?

[A] They can obtain a decree of specific performance to force Christopher to honour the contract.

[B] They can sue immediately although the time for performance has not yet arrived.

[C] They can wait until time of performance and then sue.

[D] If they accept the breach they must do all that is necessary to reduce their loss.

60. Under the Limitation Act 1980 what is the limitation period for a breach of a simple contract?

[A] 2 years.

[B] 12 years.

[C] 8 years.

[D] 6 years.

APPENDIX 1

ANSWERS TO MCT1

1.	A	16.	B	31.	C	46.	A
2.	A	17.	D	32.	A	47.	D
3.	B	18.	D	33.	C	48.	B
4.	A	19.	A	34.	C	49.	D
5.	A	20.	D	35.	D	50.	A
6.	B	21.	B	36.	A	51.	B
7.	C	22.	D	37.	C	52.	A
8.	C	23.	B	38.	A	53.	A
9.	D	24.	A	39.	C	54.	D
10.	A	25.	B	40.	C	55.	B
11.	B	26.	B	41.	A	56.	C
12.	C	27.	C	42.	C	57.	D
13.	B	28.	D	43.	D	58.	B
14.	A	29.	C	44.	A	59.	D
15.	B	30.	B	45.	C	60.	D

APPENDIX 2

ANSWERS TO MCT2

1.	C	16.	B	31.	D	46.	C
2.	C	17.	B	32.	C	47.	A
3.	B	18.	D	33.	C	48.	C
4.	C	19.	C	34.	B	49.	B
5.	C	20.	A	35.	C	50.	D
6.	D	21.	B	36.	B	51.	A
7.	C	22.	A	37.	D	52.	D
8.	A	23.	C	38.	C	53.	C
9.	C	24.	A	39.	A	54.	A
10.	C	25.	C	40.	D	55.	B
11.	B	26.	D	41.	D	56.	B
12.	B	27.	D	42.	C	57.	D
13.	A	28.	C	43.	D	58.	A
14.	B	29.	D	44.	C	59.	A
15.	C	30.	D	45.	A	60.	D

APPENDIX 3

NOTE-FORM ANSWERS TO MCT1

1. [A] is the correct answer; it is a unilateral offer. By promising that an auction is 'without reserve' an auctioneer impliedly offers to sell to the highest bidder: see *Warlow* v *Harrison* (1859) 1 E & E 309. [B] is wrong because goods on display in a shop window are an invitation to treat: see *Fisher* v *Bell* [1961] 1 QB 394. Similarly, [C] is wrong because goods offered for sale in a newspaper are also an invitation to treat: see *Partridge* v *Crittenden* [1968] 2 All ER 421. [D] is wrong because an application form for hire purchase invites you to fill it in (the invitation to treat) and then submit it to a hire purchase company asking them to 'sell' you goods on hire purchase (you are offering to buy the goods on hire purchase): see *Financings Ltd* v *Stimson* [1962] 3 All ER 386.

2. [A] is the correct answer. Letters requesting tenders are invitations to treat and therefore are not offers: see *Spencer* v *Harding* (1870) LR 5 CP 561. Answer [B] is incorrect. Since the letter requesting the bid is only an invitation to treat Lisa is under no obligation to accept a bid from one of the invitees. Answers [C] and [D] are both incorrect. Lisa's letter was a standard invitation for tenders and therefore it was not an offer: see *Spencer* v *Harding*. As a result there is no duty to accept either the highest bid or a bid from one of the four invitees.

3. [B] is the correct answer. Peter's offer to Mary is a unilateral offer which is only accepted when she does everything which was requested of her, namely, finds a client who *purchases* the house: since the house has not been sold she has not performed the stipulated act and is, therefore, entitled to nothing: see *Luxor (Eastbourne) Ltd* v *Cooper* [1941] AC 108. [A] is incorrect because Mary has not actually performed the stipulated act which was to introduce somebody who *purchases* the house. [C] is also incorrect. In *Luxor (Eastbourne) Ltd* v *Cooper* [1941] AC 108, the House of Lords refused to imply a term into the unilateral offer that the seller would not withdraw the offer at any time. [D] is also incorrect; agents in cases such as this 'take the risk' that the offer will be withdrawn and that they will be left out of pocket.

4. [A] is correct. In (i) Velma is only requesting further information – Velma is not intending to vary the terms of the original offer: see *Harvey* v *Facey* [1893] AC 552. Item (ii) could be either a counter offer or a request for further information: it depends on Velma's intention – will Zelda reasonably think that Velma is intending to keep the original offer open or that Velma really is intending to reject the original offer and replace it with her offer of £1,200; on balance it looks as if Velma's enquiry is merely a request for information: see *Stevenson, Jacque, & Co.* v *McLean* (1880) 5 QBD 346. In (iii) there is a counter offer. Zelda is varying the terms of the original offer – she is intending not to buy that which was originally offered (a car) but something different, namely, a car with a CD player: see *Hyde* v *Wrench* (1840) 3 Beav 334.

5. [A] is the correct answer. The reward is a unilateral offer. The required act of acceptance is the returning of the dog. The fact that Fred did not know of the reward when he found the dog does not matter in this case; he knew of the reward when he did the required act, i.e. when he returned the dog: see *Williams* v *Carwardine* (1833) 5 C & P 566. [B] is wrong because the £5 is promised for a past act; the only consideration for the promise of the £5 is Fred's past consideration: see *Roscorla* v *Thomas* (1842) 3 QB 234. [C] is wrong because Fred is entitled to the £20 but not the £5. [D] is wrong because this type of situation does not entitle Fred to claim on a *quantum meruit* basis, i.e. there was no expectation between the parties before the dog was returned that Fred would be rewarded for his trouble: see *Regalian Properties plc* v *London Dockland Development Corp.* [1995] 1 All ER 1005.

6. [B] is the correct answer. The general rule is acceptance must be communicated to the offeror: see *Entores Ltd* v *Miles Far East Corp.*

[1955] 2 QB 327. However, there are exceptions. If the offeree has taken all reasonable steps to communicate the acceptance and the offeror has not taken reasonable steps to ensure receiving it then the offeror is bound: see *The Brimnes* [1975] QB 929. Answer [A] is therefore incorrect. The general rule is therefore not applicable here. Answer [C] is incorrect. The offer was made by fax and therefore the acceptance can be by fax.

7. [C] is the correct answer. You might have thought that either [A] or [D] was the correct answer and that the postal rules would apply because the post would be the implied mode of communication of the acceptance from the facts. However, this would not be so in this case because Gladys's words 'that she must have notice in writing' indicates that the postal rules have been excluded and that acceptance will only take affect when she actually receives the acceptance: see *Holwell Securities Ltd* v *Hughes* [1974] 1 All ER 161. [B] is wrong because Gladys's offer will only come to an end either at the end of the 3 weeks or when she communicates the revocation of the offer to Anne.

8. [C] is the correct answer. There is no special rule that relates to communication of acceptance by telephone; the general rule applies, i.e. acceptance does not take effect until it is communicated: see *Entores Ltd* v *Miles Far East Corp.* [1955] 2 QB 327. [A] and [B] are not correct because the acceptance will only be communicated when the offeror hears the acceptance. [D] is incorrect because the contract is formed when the offeror hears the acceptance, he does not have to tell the offeree that he has heard the reply.

9. Answer [A] is incorrect. In order for Jardines to be liable the notice must be communicated to the other party: see *Entores Ltd* v *Miles Far East Corp.* [1955] 2 QB 327. This has not happened here. Answer [C] is incorrect. There are exceptions, such as where one party has taken all reasonable steps to communicate and the other party simply fails to act upon the message: see The *Brimnes* [1975] QB 929. However, in order to rely on this exception the party must have taken all reasonable steps to communicate the notice. Placing a message on an answering machine with no other form of communication is unlikely to be considered reasonable. Answer [B] is incorrect. It would be reasonable for a commercial organisation to expect such an important notice to be communicated in a more appropriate manner. Answer [D] is correct. Such notices are normally in writing and although the term mentions nothing about the mode of communication a written notice would have been more appropriate.

10. [A] is the correct answer. Phil's contract with the garage was for the service of his car and nothing else. Phil did not agree to the fitting of new tyres or the modification to his car before the garage carried them out even if he has now to agree to pay for them he would not be legally bound to pay since the garage would not be providing him with fresh consideration for his promise, only past consideration. Since past consideration is no consideration (see *Re McArdle* [1951] Ch 669) Phil will only have to pay the £60 for the service. The fact that both the tyres and modification are necessary to make the car legal and safe to drive does not give the garage the right to fit new tyres and carry out the modifications without Phil's prior agreement.

11. [B] is the correct answer. Andy and Katy have made a contract whereby Andy has agreed not to sell the horse to anyone else for a week. Katy's consideration for Andy's promise is the £50: see *Pit* v *PHH Asset Management Ltd* [1993] 4 All ER 961. [A] is wrong. There is no contract for the sale of the horse because Andy and Katy have not yet agreed a sale. [C] is wrong. Andy has not agreed to sell his horse to Katy; he has only agreed not to sell his horse to anyone else for a week. [D] is wrong; we have already seen in [B] that there is a contract between Andy and Katy.

12. [C] is the correct answer. By completing on time the plaintiff removed the need for the defendant to pay the penalty in the contract with the Housing Association. Answer [A] is not correct because Williams, in fact, did nothing more than he was contractually obliged to do. Answer [B] is not the correct ratio of the case even though, in fact, the plaintiff was not required to do more than he was required to do under the contract. Answer [D] is not correct because the issue of estoppel did not arise in the case.

13. [B] is the correct answer. [A] is true at common law (although there is a statutory exception under the Bills of Exchange Act 1882, s. 27). [B] is false. The statement should read 'Consideration must be real but need not be adequate'. [C] is true as regards the formation of a contract but is not necessary as regards the variation of a contract: see *Williams v Roffey Bros and Nicholls (Contractors) Ltd* [1991] 1 QB 1. [D] is true. English law demands that there must be consideration but is not concerned with the amount or value of the consideration.

14. [A] is the correct answer. Although a smaller sum will not discharge a larger sum because it is not of itself good accord and satisfaction. Nevertheless, a promise made in exchange for a promise to confer upon Rowan an independent benefit, that is the stamp collection, is sufficient consideration for the acceptance of the smaller sum: see *Pinnel's Case* (1602) 5 Co Rep 117. [B] is incorrect for the above reason. [C] is incorrect since the exchange of the stamp collection is consideration in support of the payment of the lesser sum, the original contract has been discharged by agreement and so there is no question that Rowan can claim the £500 because of Paul's failure to discharge. [D] is incorrect because the exchange of the stamp collection is consideration for a new contract.

15. [B] is the correct answer because it is NOT a correct statement in relation to promissory estoppel. Promissory estoppel is not a form of consideration; it is a devise by which the court will estop a party going back on their word. Although there is some room for speculation about statement [A] it seems settled at the moment that promissory estoppel can only be used to vary a pre-existing contractual relationship: see *Brikom Investments Ltd v Carr* [1979] QB 467. Statement [C] is a correct statement and is usually associated with the quote that 'promissory estoppel can only be used as a shield and not as a sword': see *Combe v Combe* [1951] 2 KB 215. [D] is also a correct statement. The important word in the statement is 'usually': see *Tool Metal Manufacturing Co. Ltd v Tungsten Electric Co. Ltd* [1955] 2 All ER 657.

16. [B] is the correct answer. Answer [C] is incorrect. The facts are similar to *Central London Property Trust Ltd v High Trees House Ltd* [1947] KB 130 where the equitable principle of promissory estoppel was developed. If one party makes a promise to the other party and that party acts upon that promise to his detriment or changes his position then the other party is prevented or estopped from going back on his word. Over the years the principle has been developed and formalised. Therefore, Jodie cannot simply change her mind. Answer [D] is incorrect. Similarly she will not be able to recover the balance owing over the last 6 months. Answer [A] is incorrect. Promissory estoppel is suspensory so that the original agreement is not extinguished by her promise. Answer [B] is correct. Provided Jodie gives reasonable notice of her intention to resume the original contract the amended terms will cease on expiration of the notice.

17. [D] is the correct answer. This problem is dealing with the area of promissory estoppel and if the necessary elements are present then Erica will be estopped from demanding the £25,000 back. Although it is sometimes said that the debtor must request the creditor to forgo part or all of the debt as is suggested in [B] it does not really matter who makes the request as long as both parties are in agreement; so [B] is wrong. [C] is also wrong because, although it is very hard luck on Erica, it would be inequitable for her to go back on her word since she intended to forgo the debt and never to recover it; this is shown by the words she uses – 'to forget the debt and to enjoy the money on a good time'. (If Philipa had forced Erica in some way to promise to forgo the £25,000 then *D & C Builders Ltd* v *Rees* [1966] 2 QB 617 would have applied and Erica would be able to reclaim her £25,000.) [A] is wrong in this particular case; Philipa would only have to show that she had provided consideration if she was trying to enforce a contract. Here she is not trying to enforce a contract but instead she is resisting Erica's claim under a contract.

18. [D] is the correct answer. Although Peter did not buy the software from Smart Accounts Ltd there is a collateral contract between himself and Smart Accounts Ltd: see *Shanklin Pier Ltd* v *Detel Products Ltd* [1951] 2 KB 854. Smart Accounts Ltd said that if Peter purchased their software from Brill Computers Ltd they 'would guarantee and maintain the software "for life"'. By Peter entering into the contract with Brill Computers Ltd he has supplied consideration for Smart Accounts Ltd's promise. Since the software does not work and Smart Accounts Ltd have refused to rectify the problem they are clearly in breach of their contractual promise.

19. [A] is the correct answer. This is the rule of privity. Third parties cannot sue or be sued on a contract: see *Tweddle* v *Atkinson* (1861) 1 B & S 393. Answer [B] is incorrect. In *Tweddle* v *Atkinson* it was held that despite the son-in-law benefiting from the contract, he could not sue upon it because he was not a party to the contract and had furnished no consideration. Answer [C] is incorrect. Third parties cannot seek protection under a contract although there are exceptions: see *Tweddle* v *Atkinson.* Answer [D] is incorrect. This is complete nonsense.

20. [D] is the correct answer. There is no difficulty with remoteness of damage. It must have been in the reasonable contemplation of the parties when they made the contract that a replacement caterer at such short notice was unlikely to be available and that therefore the reception would be terrible. [A] is incorrect. The general rule is the courts will not award damages for loss of disappointment and loss of pleasure. However, the exception is contracts mainly for pleasure. [C] is incorrect. The courts tend to limit the recovery of damages for disappointment and injured feelings to those contracts which provide for pleasure: see *Jarvis* v *Swans Tours Ltd* [1973] 1 QB 233. In *Jarvis* v *Swans Tours Ltd* Lord Denning awarded damages to both the contracting party and the members of his family. However, since the decision in *Woodar Investment Development Ltd* v *Wimpey Construction UK Ltd* [1980] 1 WLR 277 only the contracting party can recover damages for disappointment and loss of pleasure. [B] is incorrect. In *Woodar Investment Development Ltd* v *Wimpey Construction UK Ltd* it was held that only parties to the contract can recover damages. [D] is correct. In pleasure contracts where other parties have suffered, besides the contracting party, damages will be awarded on the basis that the contracting party has seen the other members suffer loss of pleasure. This approach effectively compensates the relevant members but keeps the decision within the confines of privity: see *Jackson* v *Horizon Holidays Ltd* [1975] 3 All ER 92.

21. [B] is the correct answer. The normal rule that applies to domestic agreements is that it is presumed that the parties to such an agreement do not intend to be legally bound: see *Jones* v *Padavatton* [1969] 2 All ER 616. However, this presumption is rebuttable; for example, where the normal domestic relationship has broken down: see *Merritt* v *Merritt* [1970] 2 All ER 760. As with all contracts it is, in the end, the intention of the parties that determines whether they intended to be legally bound; the test is an objective one: see *Smith* v *Hughes* (1871) LR 6 QB 597. Looking at the facts of the problem and applying the objective test it would seem that [B] is the correct answer because the normal domestic relationship seems to have broken down and, the fact that Carol and Mandy agreed through their respective solicitors to share the cost of the nursing home equally, would seem to show that they did intend to create a legal relationship.

22. [D] is the correct answer. The 'contract' is void for uncertainty. For there to be a contract there must be an agreement. What have Carolyn and John agreed to? Because a vital ingredient is missing from their agreement, namely, how many rugs are to be bought and sold, and there is no apparent way from the facts that the issue could be resolved without further agreement between the two of them their agreement is void for lack of certainty: see *May and Butcher* v *The King* [1934] 2 KB 17a.

23. [B] is the correct answer because this is NOT an effective method of determining selling price because a contract may fail for uncertainty even though offer and acceptance are present. In *Scammell* v *Ousten* [1941] AC 251 the words used in the agreement for the purchase of the van, 'on hire purchase terms', was held to be too remote. Also in *Nicolene Ltd* v *Simmonds* [1953] 1 QB 543 the court held that the phrase 'subject to usual conditions of acceptance' was too vague and therefore must be ignored. [A], [C] and [D] are effective methods because these methods can successfully be used to determine the selling price in a contract.

24. [A] is the correct answer. If goods are deemed a 'necessary', given the circumstances of that particular minor, then the contract is enforceable: see *Chapple* v *Cooper* (1844) 13 M & W 252. It is likely that the courts will take the view that one's own transport is a 'necessary' nowadays. [B] is incorrect. The contract does not become automatically enforceable on Jake reaching the age of 18. [C] is incorrect. Only if the goods are deemed necessary will the contract be enforceable. [D] is incorrect. The general rule is that contracts with minors are unenforceable, but this contract with Arnold is an exception to this rule for the reasons stated above.

25. [B] is the correct answer. However, David will be seeking specific performance of the contract which is an equitable remedy and therefore discretionary. David has taken unfair advantage of Frank and the courts are unlikely to grant him specific performance: see *Malins v Freeman* (1837) 2 Keen 25. Answer [C] is incorrect. There is a presumption that a person has capacity even if drunk. Answer [A] is incorrect. This presumption can be refuted if the intoxication is so extreme that the person fails to understand the transaction and the other party knew he did not understand: see *Gore v Gibson* (1843) 13 M & W 623. This is very difficult to establish. On these facts it is likely that he did understand but the drink lessened his resolve not to sell. Answer [D] is incorrect. Since no illegal methods were used the contract is unlikely to be set aside on the grounds of public policy.

26. [B] is the correct answer. Where all parties recognise that one party is responsible for the risk, and that responsibility by that party is customary, then the contract will bind all parties effected by it. This applies even if all relevant parties are not a party to the contract: see *Norwich City Council v Harvey* [1989] 1 All ER 1180. [C] is incorrect. It follows from the explanation to option [B] that Fred can seek protection under the contract between the council and Cowboy Ltd because the privity rule does not apply. [A] is incorrect. Fred does owe a duty of care but because of the reasons already stated he is not liable. [D] is therefore incorrect.

27. [C] is the correct answer. In *Irwin v Liverpool City Council* [1977] AC 239 the court held that it was desirable and necessary to imply a legal duty on the landlord to repair the shared parts even though no term could be implied in fact. This was implied because it was usual to have such terms between landlord and tenant. Answer [A] is incorrect. Under the officious bystanders test the clause must be so obvious to both parties that it is not worth mentioning: see *Gardner v Coutts and Co.* [1968] 1 WLR 173. This is not the case here. Answer [B] is incorrect. A term can be applied if it is considered necessary to give business efficacy to the transaction (see *Luxor (Eastbourne) Ltd v Cooper* [1941] AC 108) but this is not the case here. Answer [D] is incorrect. The standard of reasonableness is used to interpret express terms whereas the test in implied terms is whether the parties would have agreed to it.

28. [D] is the correct answer. Answers [A] and [B] are both incorrect. The traditional approach is to distinguish between a condition and a warranty. The problem here is to decide whether the lack of condition of the flat amounts to a breach of condition or a breach of warranty. On the facts it is difficult to determine because 'good order' is so vague. Where there has been a breach of a term but the effects can be major or minor the courts tend to use the more modern approach of innominate terms: see *Hongkong Fir Shipping Co. Ltd* v *Kawasaki Kisen Kaisha Ltd* [1962] 2 QB 26. Answer [C] is incorrect. The flat is not in good order but the breach is not sufficient to amount to repudiation because it could be remedied within a few days. Answer [D] is therefore correct. In the circumstances Bella would have to continue with the tenancy.

29. [C] is the correct answer. The advertisement is inviting negotiations to take place and therefore is not part of the negotiations. However, the advertisement is a misrepresentation because it is an untrue statement of fact which induced the other party to enter into the contract. Answer [A] is incorrect. The 'expert test' is one test among many which can help to decide whether a statement is a term or a representation but it is not paramount. Answer [B] is incorrect. In *Birch* v *Paramount* (1956) 16 EG 396 and *Schawel* v *Reade* [1913] 2 IR 81 it was held that only statements made during the negotiations can form part of the contact. Answer [D] is incorrect. Most advertisements are invitations to treat, with the exception of unilateral contracts where the advertisement can be the offer.

30. [B] is the correct answer. The issue is not whether the goods are, or are not, of satisfactory quality under s. 14(2) of the Sale of Goods Act 1979 (options [A] and [C]) but what was the agreement between the parties. Modgear's offer contains a condition (a condition subsequent) that Gullible can return the saucepans within 1 year if he is not entirely satisfied with them. He has exercised his right under the contract and is entitled to the full refund: see *Head* v *Tattersall* (1871) LR 7 Exch 7. [D] is incorrect because although Modgear's offer is really an invitation to treat and it is Gullible who offers to buy the saucepans from Modgear, objectively the statement about the return of the saucepans would be incorporated into the contract as a condition of the contract: see *Smith* v *Hughes* (1871) LR 6 QB 597.

31. [C] is the correct answer. The injured party in a case of negligent misrepresentation has the right to rescind the contract at common law and a right to claim damages under s. 2(1) of the Misrepresentation Act 1967. This is the case even if he has lost the right to rescission. [A] is incorrect because this is in fact a description of the remedies for fraudulent misrepresentation. [B] is incorrect because it relates to the remedy for innocent misrepresentation. [D] is incorrect because injunctions are not available as a remedy for negligent misrepresentation.

32. [A] is the correct answer. If Matthew is to succeed against Nelson he must prove that Nelson has made an operative misrepresentation that has lead him to enter into the contract. Nelson has made no such misrepresentation and is under no duty to make any representation: see *Walters v Morgan* (1861) 3 De GF & J 718. Further, silence is not a misrepresentation: see *Keates v Lord Cadogan* (1851) 10 CB 591. Since there has been no misrepresentation it follows that [B] and [D] are wrong. [C] is wrong for although there might be a mistake in the sense that a non-lawyer might use the term there is no operative mistake at law.

33. [C] is the correct answer. [A] is not correct because Peso's statement was a misrepresentation of fact which induced Zoe to enter into the contract. The question that then arises is what type of misrepresentation did Peso make? [B] might seem correct but Peso is guilty of a 'negligent' misrepresentation (option [C]) under the Misrepresentation Act 1967, s. 2 because he did not have reasonable grounds for believing the facts that he represented were true; forgetting a fact is not a reasonable ground: see *Howard Marine and Dredging Co. Ltd v A. Ogden and Sons (Excavations) Ltd* [1978] QB 574. [D] is not correct because in order to make a fraudulent misrepresentation the person who makes the misrepresentation must have a 'guilty mind'. In this problem Peso 'honestly' believes what he says; even though he might be negligent, negligence is not the same as fraud: see *Derry v Peek* (1889) 14 App Cas 337.

34. [C] is the correct answer. In order for there to be an operative misrepresentation the misled party (the representee) must have been misled by the other party (the representor) making a false statement of existing fact: see, for example, *Walters v Morgan* (1861) 3 De GF and J 718. In [A] although the shopkeeper knows that Fred is mistaken about the suitability of the drill bit the shopkeeper is not responsible for Fred's mistake. Further, the shopkeeper is under no duty to inform Fred of his mistake: see *Walter's case*. In [B] and [D]

Fred has no cause of action against the respective sellers because it was not the sellers who misled him. In [C] Chris makes a misstatement of fact (that the computer is nearly new) to Fred which induces Fred to enter into the contract; this amounts to an operative misrepresentation: see, for example, *Edgington* v *Fitzmaurice* (1885) 29 ChD 459.

35. [D] is the correct answer. At common law an operative mistake has the effect of rendering the agreement void *ab initio*. Mistake as to the existence of the subject matter at the time the parties make an agreement renders the contract void, because without the existence of the subject matter, there can be no contract: see *Strickland* v *Turner* (1852) 7 Exch 208. [C] is incorrect because voidable means valid until avoided. A voidable mistake, as in *Grist* v *Bailey* [1967] Ch 532, allows the court to treat the contract as voidable, where it is not void for mistake. This allows the court to set a contract aside whenever the parties are under a mistake of material fact. [A] is incorrect because contracts which are void from the beginning, cannot be rescinded because there is nothing to rescind. [B] is incorrect because unenforceable means that a contract exists; but cannot be enforced (special conditions apply), whereas void *ab initio* means no contract has come into being.

36. [A] is the correct answer. The leading case on unilateral mistake is *Cundy* v *Lindsay* (1878) 3 App Cas 459. Several factors must be shown in order to establish unilateral mistake. First, the identity of the other party must be essential to the innocent party to the extent that he would not have made the contract if it was with someone else. Secondly, the innocent party must establish that he only intended to contract with a real person and that he would not have made the contract on those terms if it had been with someone else. This is easier to establish if the contract is by correspondence. Answer [B] is incorrect. Where a contract is face to face the parties contract with the person in front of them and not the name of the party: see *Lewis* v *Avery* [1972] 1 QB 198. Answers [C] and [D] are both incorrect. The above judgments confirm that it is not sufficient to show that the rogue misrepresented his identity and credit worthiness.

37. [C] is the correct answer. Answer [A] is incorrect. In order to establish misrepresentation there has to be an untrue statement of fact inducing the other party to enter into the contract: see *Edgington* v *Fitzmaurice* (1885) 24 ChD 459. The car dealer correctly stated there was a maintenance agreement but did not mention that it was restrictive in its application. Answer [B] is incorrect. The general rule is that if a party signs an agreement they are bound whether or not they have read the agreement: see *L'Estrange* v *Graucob* [1934] 2 KB 394. Answer [C] is correct. However, there are exceptions. Under the principle of *non est factum* a person must show that the deed signed was fundamentally different to the one agreed. Only then will the contract be avoided: see *Saunders* v *Anglia Building Society* [1971] AC 1004. Beryl cannot establish *non est factum* because the document she signed was not fundamentally different from what was agreed. Answer [D] is incorrect. In certain circumstances a contract can be rescinded even if the contract has been signed. Examples are misrepresentation, *non est factum* and statutory exceptions.

38. [A] is the correct answer. It applies whenever the relationship between the parties is such that one is by reason of confidence reposed in him by the other, able to take unfair advantage of that other: see *Tate* v *Williamson* (1866) LR 2 Ch App 55. There is little here to suggest 'independent will': see *Inche Noriah* v *Shaikh Allie Bin Omar* [1929] AC 127. [B] is incorrect. Traditionally duress is restricted to actual or threatened physical violence to, or unlawful constraint of the person contracting: see *Cumming* v *Ince* (1847) 11 QB 112. [C] is incorrect. The law relating to mistake is quite complicated. Ken is bound by his signature unless he is mistaken as to the identity or nature of the document as signed, in which case he may claim, *non est factum* [D] is incorrect. Statements of opinion are 'mere puffs' and as such are not actionable misrepresentations. Here, as in *Bissett* v *Wilkinson* [1927] AC 177, Rosemary has no personal knowledge of the facts on which the statement was based.

39. [C] is the correct answer. Answer [D] is incorrect. On the facts Jill would recover some of her capital because the amount owing on the mortgage is less than the value of the house. Answer [A] is incorrect. Jill will have to show undue influence on the basis that she reposed trust and confidence in David because of their relationship: see *Bank of Credit and Commerce International SA* v *Aboody* [1992] 4 All ER 955. In order for Jill to recover all the £30,000 she will have show undue influence as between herself and the bank. In *Barclays Bank plc* v *O'Brien* [1994] 1 AC 180 it was held that a creditor must have notice or constructive notice of the relationship. On the facts this is unlikely since the purchase was made in David's name. Therefore, the bank's charge against the property is enforceable. Jill will not be able to recover any sums from the bank. Answer [B] is incorrect. Since undue influence is an equitable doctrine and it is not possible to restore the parties to their original position due to the loss of value in the house, the court will look at what is fair and just in the circumstances when dividing the net capital: see *Cheese* v *Thomas* [1994] 1 WLR 129. On these facts it would not be fair to split the net sale proceeds equally. Answer [C] is correct. David was at fault in not paying the mortgage and since undue influence is an equitable doctrine, Jill is likely to recover most or all of the net sale proceeds.

40. [C] is the correct answer. The leading case on undue influence and its effect on lenders is *Barclays Bank plc* v *O'Brien* [1994] 1 AC 180. If a lender is on notice that the loan gives the surety no benefit, then the lender must take reasonable steps to ensure that the surety has been informed of the consequences of the loan by receiving independent advice. The solicitors were instructed by the bank to act for them and give independent advice to Jean. Answer [B] is incorrect because the bank has avoided constructive notice by instructing solicitors to give independent advice. Answer [A] is incorrect. Third parties are not bound by untrue statements unless the third party has constructive notice. Answer [D] is incorrect. The bank avoided constructive notice by instructing independent solicitors to advise. Signing documents is not sufficient in itself to avoid undue influence.

41. [A] is the correct answer. The contract is formed when Eric enters the car park: see *Thornton* v *Shoe Lane Parking Ltd* [1971] 2 QB 163. [B] is incorrect because the stamped ticket would not be considered a contractual document and therefore it would not be capable of incorporating terms into any contract between Eric and the car park company: see *Chapelton* v *Barry UDC* [1940] 1 KB 532. [C] is incorrect because the contract was already formed when Eric entered into the car park; the exclusion clause would therefore be brought to Eric's attention too late to be incorporated into the contract: see *Olley* v *Marlborough Court Ltd* [1949] 1 KB 532. [D] is incorrect because the exclusion clause was incorporated into the contract between Eric and the car park owner at the car park entrance.

42. [C] is *incorrect* and is the right answer. Under sch. 1 of the Unfair Terms in Consumer Contracts Regulations 1994, they apply to all terms of the contract except terms defining the main subject matter and price provided these terms are in plain and intelligible language. Answer [A] is correct. Regulation 3 of the 1994 Regulations confirms that the Regulations apply to all contracts where one party deals as a consumer and the contract has not been individually negotiated, subject to a few express exceptions. Answer [B] is correct. When comparing the definition of reasonableness under sch. 2 of the Unfair Contract Terms Act 1977 and the definition of 'fairness' in sch. 3 of the 1994 Regulations, they appear to be similar but it is for the courts to decide if they are the same. Answer [D] is correct. Regulation 2 defines a consumer as 'a natural person'.

43. Answer [A] is incorrect. The Unfair Contract Terms Act 1977 applies to most contracts containing clauses which either restrict or exclude liability but not all. The Act does not apply to contracts made between parties where neither are acting in the course of a business. Answer [B] is incorrect. In consumer contracts some clauses are void but most are subject to the test of reasonableness: see s. 11 of the Unfair Contract Terms Act 1977. Answer [C] is incorrect. Clauses excluding liability for personal injury and death because of negligence are void: see s. 2 of the Unfair Contract Terms Act 1977. Answer [D] is correct. Where the buyer is not a consumer and the contract is not on standard terms and the party relying on the exclusion clause is not attempting to exclude liability under the implied terms the Act does not apply.

44. [A] is the correct answer. On terms other than exclusion clauses, the courts take a liberal approach in interpreting words. The courts will look at the intention of the parties and the reasonable man test to determine its meaning. A policyholder reading such a clause would assume that the policy covers all responsibilities, not just legal duties. The courts are likely to take the same view. Answer [D] is incorrect. This clause is simply defining the cover under the policy and is therefore not an exclusion clause. Answer [C] is incorrect. The Unfair Contract Terms Act 1977 only applies to exclusion clauses. Answer [B] is incorrect. If the insurance company intended to restrict the policy to legal responsibilities then this must be clearly stated.

45. [C] is the correct answer. Anything which is ambiguous or unclear in an exclusion clause will, at common law, 'be construed against he who seeks to rely upon it'. Accordingly, where a clause fails to deal with a specific matter it will not be deemed to cover that matter: see *Lee and Son (Grantham) Ltd* v *Railways Executive* [1949] 2 All ER 581; see also *Wallis Son and Wells* v *Pratt and Hayes* [1911] AC 394. [A] and [D] are true but they do not relate to the rules which apply to the *contra proferentem* rule. [B] is incorrect. It is confusing and not strictly true, since in many consumer contracts an exclusion clause is affected by the operation of the Unfair Contract Terms Act 1977 and as such may be rendered void. Under the Unfair Contract Terms Act 1977 and the Unfair Terms in Consumer Contracts Regulations 1994 many other terms have to satisfy the 'reasonableness test' in order to be binding.

46. [A] is the correct answer. [B] and [C] are wrong because there has been no breach of contract by Sheering. Professional footballers are prone to receive this type of injury and it is within the contemplation of the parties that this will happen from time to time without any form of liability attaching to the footballer. [D] is incorrect because the injury is not sufficient to bring to an end the commercial purpose of the contract; Sheering will still be available to play football for Oldfortress City for the rest of the season: see *Davis Contractors Ltd* v *Fareham UDC* [1956] 2 All ER 145 where Lord Radcliffe said 'There must be . . . such a change in the significance of the obligation that the thing undertaken would, if performed, be a different thing from that contracted for'. Sheering's injury would not make his performance of the contract 'a different thing from that contracted for'.

47. [D] is the correct answer because this is *not* a definition of frustration. If the event was foreseen, or should have been foreseen by one party but not by the other, that party cannot rely on frustration: see *Walton Harvey Ltd* v *Walker and Homfroy Ltd* [1931] 1 Ch 274. [A] is the incorrect answer because this is a definition of frustration of contract. In *Krell* v *Henry* [1905] 2 KB 740 the Court of Appeal held that the doctrine of frustration applied when a 'state of things' essential to the contract fails to come into existence. [B] is also an incorrect answer because this is a definition of frustration which is similar to that found in [A]. [C] is an incorrect answer because this is a definition of frustration. A contract becomes impossible to perform in one of three ways: (i) destruction of the subject matter as in *Taylor* v *Caldwell* (1863) 3 B & S 826; (ii) death of a party; and (iii) unavailability of subject matter: see *Jackson* v *Union Marine Insurance Co. Ltd* (1874) LR 10 CP 125.

48. [B] is the correct answer. Suspension by the governing body is an illustration of discharge by frustration; but is a rare event as can be seen from *Re Shipton, Anderson & Co.* [1915] 3 KB 676. [A] is incorrect because the substitution of a Ford GT 40 in place of the Lola T70 does not amount to discharge by frustration since it is self induced as in *Maritime National Fishery* v *Ocean Trawlers* [1953] AC 524. [C] is incorrect because the transfer of the race to Castle Combe is not a frustrating event. As Viscount Simmonds stated in *Tsakiroglou* v *Noblee Thorl Gmbh* [1961] AC 93: 'the doctrine of frustration must be applied within a very narrow limit'. Since the race can go ahead at Castle Combe it is not frustrated. [D] is incorrect for the same reasons as stated in [A].

49. [D] is the correct answer. The 'blue pencil test' will be applied by the court only to sever an illegal promise if this can be done by cutting words out of the contract. This has been called the 'blue pencil test' because it must be possible to sever by simply running a pencil through the offending words. The courts will not redraft, or reword, or add new words, or substitute words: see *Mason* v *Provident Clothing and Supply Co. Ltd* [1913] AC 724. [A] is incorrect because it relates to a test applied by the courts to determine whether the restraint of trade may be justified. [B] is incorrect because again it relates to a method of assessing whether the restraint is unreasonable: see *Fitch* v *Dewes* [1921] 2 AC 158 and *Scorer* v *Seymour-Johns* [1966] 1 WLR 1419. [C] is incorrect because this is a method used to establish that even where it is reasonable such a restraint will still not apply if it is against public policy: see *Herbert Morris Ltd* v *Saxelby* [1916] AC 688. Again this has nothing to do with the severance of the illegal promise.

50. [A] is the correct answer because the relationship between a company and its director is not one of utmost good faith. The relationship appears to fall short of this, although the Companies Act 1985 does attempt to establish a number of rules requiring a director to disclose any personal interest he may have in a contract: see s.

317 of the Companies Act 1985, *Boston Deep Sea Fishing Co.* v *Ansell* (1888) 39 ChD 339 and *Cooks* v *Deeks* [1916] AC 554. [B] is incorrect. A contract of insurance is a contract of utmost good faith. This requires that the party who signs such a contract must disclose the whole truth. [C] and [D] are incorrect because they are situations in which the principle of utmost good faith has been created.

51. [B] is the correct answer. An agreement such as this is both void and illegal at common law. Generally property transferred under a void contract is recoverable; but if the agreement is also illegal it is not usually recoverable: see *Taylor* v *Chester* (1869) LR 4 QB 309. If a seller sues for the recovery of goods delivered under an illegal contract he will fail, for to justify his claim he must necessarily disclose his own legal position. However, one of two legal exceptions operates, one of which offers relief where one party is much less at fault than the other, and where he has been induced by fraud to enter into an illegal contract: see *Hughes* v *Liverpool Victoria Legal Friendly Society* [1916] 2 KB 482. [A] is incorrect. George cannot recover on the grounds of the contract being void because it was also illegal at inception. [D] is incorrect because for a *quantum meruit* to succeed the contract must be lawful at inception. The maxim *in pari delicto potior e'st conditio defendentis* applies and the defendant may keep what he has given: see *Chettiar* v *Chettiar* [1962] AC 294.

52. [A] is the correct answer. Jock could have claimed that the contract was discharged by breach in February. By agreeing to the end of April Jock had waived that right. The waiver may be oral, written or inferred from conduct, even where the contract itself is one which is required by law to be in or evidenced in writing: see *Besseler, Waechter, Glover & Co.* v *South Derwent Coal Co. Ltd* [1938] 1 KB 408. Once the promise has been acted upon Jack cannot afterwards go back on his word. Although a waiver, as here, is similar to a promissory estoppel, as it produces the same result, there is authority for the view that the doctrines must be kept distinct: see *Brikom Investments* v *Carl* [1979] QB 467. However, his notice requiring completion by the end of May establishes that time is *now* of the essence: see *Rickards (Charles)* v *Oppenheim* [1950] 1 KB 616. [B] is incorrect. Clearly there has been no consent here and there is no agreement. [C] is incorrect because a shortage of labour is not a frustrating event: see *Davis Contractors Ltd* v *Fareham Urban District Council* [1956] 2 All ER 145. [D] is incorrect because late completion of the work is not performance since the contract has been discharged by breach.

53. [A] is the correct answer. Mearl's Performance Parts will only be liable for normal loss of business profits as can be seen from *Victoria Laundry (Windsor) Ltd* v *Newman Industries* [1949] 2 KB 528. [B] is incorrect because such a claim for special or abnormal damages will only succeed when at the time of contracting the defendant was aware of the likely loss which would result from the breach of contract. This can be seen from a more recent application of the principle inherent in the *Victoria Laundry* case; in *Balfour Beatty Construction (Scotland) Ltd* v *Scottish Power, The Times*, 23 March 1994, the House of Lords limited such claims for damages to those of normal loss. [C] is incorrect because such losses are not too remote. [D] is incorrect because it is unlikely such loss was within the contemplation of the parties at the time they contracted as can be seen from *H. Parson (Livestock) Ltd* v *Uttley Ingham* [1978] 1 All ER 525.

54. [D] is the correct answer. It is rebutable here because a clause will be a liquidated damage clause where it is impossible to determine the actual loss incurred, provided it is not too excessive. Toby had a reputation of producing outstanding quality components. Herman would have damaged this reputation and which could result in loss of orders in the long term. Answer [A] is incorrect. The courts make a distinction between liquidated damage clauses which are enforceable and penalty clauses which are not enforceable. Answer [B] is incorrect. In *Dunlop Pneumatic Tyre Co. Ltd* v *New Garage and Motor Co.* [1915] AC 79 the court laid down rules for determining whether a clause is a liquidated damage clause or penalty clause. There is a presumption that where the same amount is to be paid upon the happening of more or several events that the clause is a penalty clause and therefore void but this is rebutable. Answer [C] is incorrect. The courts will not normally vary such a clause.

55. [B] is the correct answer. The test to be applied is whether Anna's loss is within the reasonable contemplation of both parties: see *Hadley* v *Baxendale* (1854) 9 Exch 341. Issac clearly would have contemplated that Anna was a commercial grower and that if the air conditioning system broke down her plants would be lost. Answer [A] is incorrect. Anna did not inform Issac of the lucrative contract and therefore this is not in reasonable contemplation: see *Hadley v Baxendale*. Anna is not entitled to the additional £20,000. Answer [D] is incorrect. Issac clearly is in breach of contract since his defective workmanship caused the loss of the plants. Anna is entitled to some compensation. Answer [C] is incorrect. Parties cannot recover for both loss of and capital expenditure. The plaintiff must claim one or the other because otherwise the innocent party is compensated twice: *Cullinane v British 'Rema' Manufacturing Co. Ltd* [1954] 1 QB 292.

56. [C] is the correct answer because these statements accurately demonstrate the true position. Statement (i) demonstrates the wide view of interpretation taken in the *Suisse Atlantique Société d'Armement Maritime SA v Rotterdamsche Kolen Centrale* [1967] 1 AC 361. Here the innocent party is entitled to treat the contract as repudiated and to rescind the contract. When the breach is less dramatic a more narrow construction is placed on the injured parties position: see *Charter House Credit Co. Ltd v Tolly* [1963] 2 QB 683. Statement (ii) is correct because the injured party is entitled to either affirm the breach or accept it: see *Charter House Credit Co. Ltd v Tolley*. Statement (iii) is correct because no positive affirmation is required: see *Wathes (Western) Ltd v Austin (Menswear) Ltd* [1967] 1 AC 395. *Note*: Some exclusion clauses will however cover the fundamental breach: see *Photo Production Ltd v Securicor Transport Ltd* [1980] 1 All ER 556. Statement (iv) is incorrect because damages alone would be an adequate remedy in these circumstances.

57. [D] is the correct answer. The award of damages is to ensure that a party who has suffered a loss as a result of another party's breach of contract should be put into the position he would have been in had the contract been performed. [A] is incorrect because damages are a civil remedy and not a criminal remedy. [B] is incorrect because the aim of damages is not to guarantee that the defaulting party does not profit from the breach: see *Teacher v Calder* [1889] 1 ChD 39 and *Surrey County Council v Bredero Homes Ltd* [1993] 1 WLR 1361. In awarding damages the court will ensure that injured parties do not make a profit: see *Lake v Bayliss* [1974] 1 WLR 1073. [C] is incorrect because damages, as such, do not ensure that acts performed by the injured party will be paid for. *Note*: In cases where the injured party has performed, under the contract, work, the value of which exceeds what would have been due to him if the contract had been fully performed, then he may claim on a *quantum meruit*, the value of that work already done if the other party is in breach of contract. Such a claim will be quasi-contractual.

58. [B] is the correct answer. [A] is wrong because the doctrine of substantial performance does not state that the full price has to be paid; the innocent party can make a deduction from the price which represents the cost of remedying the defect in the other's performance of the contract: see *H. Dakin and Co. Ltd* v *Lee* [1916] 1 KB 566. [C] and [D] are wrong because Fantastic Car Builders have substantially performed the contract and therefore Rob must pay the majority of the £300,000 immediately.

59. [D] is correct. Guns Unlimited cannot sue Steve for refusing to take the gun on 1 December because the contract for the sale of the gun was frustrated on 5 November when the government introduced the law outlawing the sale or possession of handguns: see *Avery* v *Bowden* (1855) 5 E & B 714. [A] is incorrect. Steve's anticipatory repudiatory breach of 1 October entitled Guns Unlimited to accept his breach and to sue him immediately for his breach: see *Hochster* v *De La Tour* (1853) 2 E & B 678. However, Guns Unlimited waived their right to treat the contract as repudiated: see *White and Carter (Councils) Ltd* v *McGregor* [1962] AC 413. The same analysis applies to [B].

60. [D] is the correct answer. An anticipatory breach or repudiation occurs when one party, either expressly or by implication, indicates that he does not intend to be bound by an agreement. Here the injured party is entitled to sue immediately: see *Hochester* v *De La Tour* (1853) 2 E & B 678 and *Frost* v *Knight* (1872) LR 7 Ex 111. [A] is incorrect because the injured party is not under any obligation to wait until the date fixed for performance before commencing his action; but he may immediately treat the contract as at an end and sue for damages. [B] is incorrect because where one party commits a repudiatory anticipatory breach, the other party, the innocent party, can sue at once, and need not wait for the contract date of performance to arrive, even where his right is contingent on the occurrence of some other event: see *Frost* v *Knight* (1872) LR 7 Ex 111. [C] is incorrect because the injured party need not wait for the contract date of performance to come round: see the *Hochester* case. *Note*: the doctrine of anticipatory breach does not apply in the case of a time charterparty. Here failure to pay cannot amount to anticipatory repudiation: see *Afouos Shipping Co. SA v Romano Pagnan* [1983] 1 WLR 195.

APPENDIX 4

NOTE-FORM ANSWERS TO MCT2

1. [C] is the correct answer. Max's offer is a unilateral offer. Fred accepts the offer when, knowing of the offer, he does all that was requested of him. This he has done; he knew of the reward and gave the required information and that information resulted in the criminal conviction of Jane. [A] is incorrect because although Fred has given the information to Max the offer of the reward was for information 'leading to a criminal conviction'. Since Jane was acquitted Fred did not do all that the unilateral offer required him to do. [B] is probably incorrect on the authorities as they are. *Neville* v *Kelly* (1862) 12 CBNS 740 and *Gibbons* v *Proctor* (1891) 64 LT 594 support the view that it does not matter if the person giving the information *does not know* of the reward but *Fitch* v *Snedaker* (1868) 38 NY 248 and *R* v *Clarke* (1927) 40 CLR 227 seem to support the opposite view. [D] is incorrect on the authorities as they are. In *England* v *Davidson* (1840) 11 Ad & El 856, a similar case to the facts of the problem, it was argued that the contract was against public policy but the court rejected the argument.

2. [C] is the correct answer. Both (i) and (ii) are wrong because although unilateral offers are commonly made to large groups of people (as in *Carlill* v *Carbolic Smoke Ball Co.* [1893] 1 QB 256) the number of people to whom an offer is made is irrelevant. What makes an offer a unilateral offer is the way in which it is accepted. If in order to accept an offer the offeree has to complete an act that has been requested by the offeror and the offeror requires no notification that the act has been completed then the offer is a unilateral offer: see the *Carlill* case. Item (iii) is wrong because a unilateral offer, just like any other offer, can be revoked in the right circumstances. The issue that sometimes arises in the case of unilateral offers is whether a unilateral offer can be revoked once the offeree has started the required act but before the offeree has completed the act: compare, for example, *Errington v Errington and Woods* [1952] 1 KB 290 with *Luxor (Eastbourne) Ltd v Cooper* [1941] AC 108.

3. [B] is the correct answer. Although Simon had agreed to keep his offer open for a week he was not contractually bound to keep it open for the week; he could revoke his offer within the week provided he communicated his revocation to Wendy before she accepted his offer. The issue, then, is had Simon revoked his offer before Wendy purported to accept it? [A] is incorrect because the postal rules do not apply to revocations; Simon's revocation will only take effect when it is actually communicated to Wendy on 7 October: see *Byrne v Van Tienhoven* (1880) 5 CPD 344. [C] would be correct were it not for the fact that Simon's revocation has been effectively communicated to Wendy by her best friend Carol on 6 October: see *Dickinson v Dodds* (1876) 2 ChD 463. [D] is incorrect since there is no contract between Simon and Wendy for him to break.

4. [C] is incorrect and the right answer because the postal rules only apply to acceptances sent by post when the post is the anticipated mode of communication of the acceptance; the postal rules do not apply to counter-offers. A counter-offer would only take effect when it was actually communicated to the offeror. [A] is correct because once an offer has been accepted the contract is formed and the offer ceases to exist. [B] is correct because if the offeror makes an offer but fixes no time limit as to when it is to lapse then the offer will lapse after a reasonable time. [D] is correct because although the death of the offeror may, or may not, depending on the circumstances of the case, bring an offer to an end the death of the offeree will always bring an offer to an end: see *Reynolds v Atherton* (1921) 125 LT 690.

5. [C] is the correct answer. [A] is quite clearly wrong: *Pharmaceutical Society of Great Britain v Boots Cash Chemists (Southern) Ltd* [1952] 2 QB 795, established that the contract of sale came into existence at the cash desk, up until that point no offer has been made. The offer is made by the buyer to the seller when the buyer presents the goods to the seller ([B]): see the *Boots* case. The scanning of the goods ([C]) would seem to be Tesbury's acceptance of Mary's offer to buy the goods. Mary's paying for the goods ([D]) would be her performance of her obligation under the contract.

6. [D] is the correct answer. An e-mail will probably be treated as an instantaneous form of communication and therefore the postal rules will not apply; therefore [A] is wrong: see *Entores Ltd v Miles Far East Corporation* [1955] 2 QB 327. [B] is wrong because the e-mail sent at 12.00 hours was not a counter-offer; it was an acceptance of the offer – coupled with an offer to buy more sides of beef. [C] is incorrect because the Macburgers plc had accepted Beef Supplies plc offer at 12.30 hours which was one hour before Beef Supplies plc will be estopped from asserting that they did not read the e-mail at 12.30 hours which was during their normal office hours: see *The Brimnes, Tenax Steamship Co. Ltd v Owners of the motor vessel Brimnes* [1974] 3 All ER 88 .

7. [C] is correct because as far as Sally is concerned Peter's offer is still open because she is accepting within the 10 days, Peter has not communicated the revocation of his offer to her and Sally does not know that the car has been sold. [A] is wrong because Peter's offer remains open until the time limit expires or he communicates the revocation of his offer to Sally. Merely selling the car to someone else does not bring the offer to an end: see *Adams v Lindsell* (1818) 1 B & Ald 681. [B] is wrong because the offer was brought to an end when Sally learnt that the car had been sold: see *Dickinson v Dodds* (1876) 2 ChD 463. Sally could now sue Peter for breach of his contractual promise to keep his offer open for 10 days but his offer to sell his car to her no longer exists: see *Routledge v Grant* (1828) 4 Bing 653. [D] is incorrect because Peter has not made a misstatement of fact which has induced Sally to enter into a contract.

8. [A] is the correct answer. This question is similar to the *Blackpool and Fylde Aero Club Ltd v Blackpool Borough Council* [1990] 1 WLR 1195. It was held in the *Blackpool* case that a collateral contract can come into existence to the extent that if one party complies with their terms of invitation, the other party has a duty to consider the bid. Rabbit Ltd are liable to that extent. Answer [B] is incorrect. The general rule is that the request for tenders are invitations to treat in relation to the actual proposed contract: see *Spencer v Harding* (1870)

LR 5 CP 561. But in certain circumstances a collateral contract can be created. Answer [C] is incorrect. As already explained requests for tenders are not normally offers. Answer [D] is incorrect. Rabbit Ltd cannot avoid liability simply because the contract has been offered to someone else. A party can still be liable even if they contract with someone else.

9. [C] is the correct answer. Item (i) is not a correct statement because communication of the acceptance is not a requirement in unilateral contracts: see *Carlill* v *Carbolic Smoke Ball Co.* [1893] 1 QB 256. Item (ii) is correct because whatever the type of contract, intention to create legal relations must be shown; this is even the case in unilateral contracts. In the *Carlill* case the fact that the Carbolic Smokeball Co. had deposited money with a bank showed that they did intend to create legal relations. Item (iii) is incorrect because consideration is not required where the contract is made by deed.

10. [C] is the correct answer. In this type of case where tenders are invited for the supply of 'such quantities of fuel oil as may be required . . .' the successful tenderor in fact makes what amounts to a standing offer to the offeree (the university in this case): see *Great Northern Rly Co.* v *Witham* (1873) LR 9 CP 16. The university accepts the standing offer when it places a particular order. So, in this case, the university has accepted the offer for the March oil and Slick Oil Ltd is bound to supply that oil. However, Slick Oil Ltd can withdraw its standing offer by communicating its revocation to the university: see the *Witham* case above. Therefore, [A] is wrong because there is no such contract between the university and Slick Oil Ltd. [B] is wrong because the university's March order was an acceptance of Slick Oil Ltd's standing offer. [D] is wrong because Slick Oil Ltd can withdraw its standing offer.

11. [B] is the correct answer. Executed consideration is consideration that has been performed, i.e. it is not still at the 'promissory' stage. In [A] both parties have yet to perform their part of the contract therefore both parties' consideration is still executory. In [B] the executed consideration is that part of Colin's promise that he has performed, i.e. the first instalment that he has paid. In [C] there is no contract since there was no understanding that Tony was to be paid for washing Ingrid's car. In [D] although Martin should have performed his part of the contract by giving his racket to Rob last week he failed so to do so – his consideration is still executory although it should have been executed by this time.

12. [B] is the correct answer. The consideration given by the plaintiff was that they caused the contractors to enter into the contract with the defendant (in the main contract for the purchase of the paint). The plaintiff was suing on the collateral contract (*Plaintiff* v *Defendant* as to specification of paint). The court accepted that the defendant had induced the plaintiff to specify the paint manufactured by the defendant. Accordingly [A] is incorrect. [C] is incorrect because the *ratio* did not discuss the possibility of the contractors being viewed as the defendant's agents. [D] is incorrect because this was not mentioned in the *ratio* of the case. In fact counsel for the defendant acknowledged that a warranty could stand side by side with the main contract.

13. [A] is the correct answer. The issue raised by this problem is whether Ted has agreed to furnish fresh consideration to Freda and Gretta or has he done no more than he was already contractually bound to do? Since Gretta was not a party to the original contract between Ted and Freda when Ted agrees with Gretta to deliver the barley to her for £200 that is a new agreement between the two of them which is supported on both sides by fresh consideration. Ted's agreement to deliver the goods to Gretta is his promise to her; it is a new consideration as between the two of them: see *Scotson* v *Pegg* (1861) 6 H & N 295. As regards the £100, Ted's fresh consideration is his agreement to deliver part of the wheat at a date earlier than he was obliged to do under his original contract with Freda: *Pinnel's case* (1602) 5 Co Rep 117a.

14. [B] is the correct answer. In *Foakes* v *Beer* (1884) 9 App Cas 605, there was no satisfaction and so the promise to take less than was owing was unenforceable. Answer [A] is not correct. This case is authority for the principle of promissory estoppel. Answer [C] is not correct. In *Welby* v *Drake* (1825) 1 C & P 557, it was held that payment by a third party was satisfaction of a debt of another person. Answer [D] is not correct. This is authority for the proposition that promissory estoppel is a shield and not a sword.

15. [C] is the correct answer. Although everybody remembers the *High Trees* case as the case that first established the principle of promissory estoppel (cf. *Hughes* v *Metropolitan Railway Co.* (1887) 2 App Cas 439) Denning J, as he then was, only made his comments about promissory estoppel *obiter*. In fact the landlord only sued for the last two quarters' rent and he won his case. Therefore, [A], [B] and [D] are wrong.

16. [B] is correct, as it is the most accurate description of a condition precedent. A condition precedent governs the order in which contracting parties must perform their obligations under their contract. Such a condition stipulates that one party is under no obligation what so ever to perform his side of the bargin until the other party has performed his side of the bargin: see *Société Générale de Paris* v *Milders* (1883) 49 LT 55. [A] is incorrect because this is a term providing for 'liquidated damages' in the event of a breach of contract. [C] is incorrect because this is a definition of a condition subsequent. [D] is incorrect because no breach of a contractual term has the effect of *automatically* discharging a contract.

17. [B] is *incorrect* and the right answer. This was the decision by Lord Denning in *Jackson* v *Horizon Holidays Ltd* [1975] 1 WLR 1468. However, Lord Denning's approach was rejected in *Woodar Investment Development Ltd* v *Wimpey Construction Co. Ltd* [1980] 1 WLR 277. The present view is that third parties cannot claim damages on contracts where only the third parties have suffered loss. Answer [A] is correct. Only a party to the contract can claim specific performance for the benefit of the third party: see, for example, *Beswick* v *Beswick* [1968] AC 58. Answer [C] is correct. This is an exception which is applied narrowly. There must be an intention to create a trust and an intention to benefit a third party. In practice it is difficult to imply a trust unless the intention is express: see *Green* v *Russell* [1959] 2 QB 266. Answer [D] is correct. It would be difficult for the law of agency to operate within the doctrine of privity.

18. [D] is the correct answer. Mere commercial pressure is not sufficient to set aside a contract: see *The Siboen and the Sibotre* [1976] Lloyd's Rep 293. However, where the threat prevents a voluntary agreement to the new terms this can amount to economic duress: see *Universe Tankships Inc. of Monrovia* v *International Transport*

Workers' Federation (The Universe Sentinel) [1983] 1 AC 366. In the circumstances Norma had no choice but to pay the increase in price and therefore this will probably amount to economic duress. [A] is incorrect. Simply because Norma agreed to the new price does not mean that she cannot recover the extra payment. Once the terms of a contract have been agreed the terms cannot be varied unless fresh consideration is supplied: see *Stilk v Myrick* (1809) 2 Camp 317. [B] is incorrect. Duress is limited to actual physical or threatened violence. [C] is incorrect. In *Williams v Roffery Bros and Nicholls (Contractors) Ltd* [1991] 1 QB 1 the court held that a promise to complete on time can amount to fresh consideration if the other party receives a benefit from it provided the new agreement was not made under economic duress.

19. [C] is the correct answer. Although in [A] the parties still have to agree a fundamental term between themselves which would normally be fatal to the formation of a contract (see *May and Butcher v The King* [1934] 2 KB 17a) because they have provided for a third party to agree the price should they fail to so do, then the contract will not lack certainty: see *Foley v Classique Coaches Ltd* [1934] 2 KB 1. [B] results in a valid contract because although the arbitration clause is vague in that the second part of it talks of 'any other dispute in New York' the court will ignore these words as meaningless and will give effect to the rest of the contract: see *Lovelock v Exportles* [1968] 1 Lloyd's Rep 163. [C] is the correct answer and will not result in a contract because its terms are too vague. Both parties have never dealt with each other before and it is not possible to determine what the usual hire purchase terms are; there cannot be any usual terms between them: see *Scammell v Ouston* [1941] AC 251. [D] does result in a contract. Where all of the main terms in a contract have been agreed, and the parties have agreed to be bound by them the fact that further terms are to be negotiated will not prevent there from being a concluded contract: see *Pagnan Spa v Feed Products Ltd* [1987] 2 Lloyd's Rep 601.

20. [A] is the correct answer. The wording of the question is somewhat misleading. We frequently talk about contracts which are void. Strictly speaking there is no such creature as a void contract; if it is void a contract does not come into existence. [B], [C] and [D] are all wrong because they all presuppose that there is a contract in existence and there is not if the agreement lacks certainty.

21. [B] is the correct answer. Parties may make an agreement by which they expressly declare that it is not to be binding in law. If such a declaration is made it will, like other express agreements, be accepted by the courts: see *Jones v Vernon's Pools Limited* [1938] 2 ALL ER 626 and *Rose and Frank v Crompton* [1925] AC 445. [A] is incorrect because this merely creates a speciality contract and would not make their agreement unenforceable. [C] is incorrect because this is a method by which a simple agreement is created. [D] is incorrect because only certain types of contract have to be witnessed and this is not one of them.

22. [A] is the correct answer. The assumption from *Balfour v Balfour* [1919] 2 KB 571 and *Meritt v Meritt* [1970] 1 WLR 1211 is that a social domestic agreement does not give rise to legal relations unless there is express written evidence to the contrary. [B] is incorrect because social domestic agreements are presumed not to be legally binding: see *Jones v Padavatton* [1969] 2 All ER 616. [C] is incorrect because no legal intention exists and none can be implied. Agreements for the sale of land are commonly made 'subject to contract'. These words negative contractual intention, so that the parties are not normally bound until the formal contracts are exchanged: see *Frank Co. v J.R. Crompton and Bros* [1923] 2 KB 261. [D] is incorrect because again it is a purely social and domestic situation.

23. [C] is the correct answer. Provided the only dispute concerning the validity of the contract is to do with Jim being a minor the guarantee will be enforceable as against Jim's mother. This is because s. 2 of the Minors Act 1987 says guarantees are valid where the principal contract is with a minor and the only dispute as to its enforceability is connected with the fact that one party is a minor.

24. [A] is the correct answer. Trade practice and usage may be implied into a contract in the absence of a usual or common course of dealing: see *British Crane Hire Corporation Ltd v Ipswich Plant Hire Ltd* [1974] 2 WLR 856. The case, however, did not place much stress on the course of dealings but rather on the common understanding between the parties, namely, that the hiring was to be on the terms of the plaintiff's usual conditions. Terms implied by trade and custom can also be implied in order to give 'business efficacy' to an agreement because it is deficient in some way: see *The Moorcock* (1889) 14 PD

64 and *Brown and Davis Ltd* v *Galbraith* [1972] 1 WLR 997. Further, when express terms are clear and unambiguous, the court will only imply a term if it is clear that the parties must have intended it to form part of the contract: see *Trollope and Colls* v *NW Metropolitan Regional Hospital Board* [1973] 1 WLR 601. [B] is incorrect because the courts will not imply a term into a contract so as to replace an unusual term. [C] is incorrect because the court will not imply a term to provide for events not originally contemplated at the time of the agreement. It follows that [D] is incorrect.

25. [C] is the correct answer. Answer [A] is incorrect. Smelly Perfume cannot end the contract simply because Josie is in breach of a term in the contract. The classification of the term will determine whether the breach is sufficient to repudiate the contract. Terms are classified into conditions, warranties and innominate terms. Answer [B] is incorrect. The court will not hold a clause in a contract to be a term simply because the contract says its a condition: see *Schuler AG* v *Wickman Machine Tools Sales Ltd* [1973] 2 All ER 39. [C] is the correct answer. The clause could be classified as either a warranty or an innominate term. The contract stipulates that the clause is a condition but the court could take the view that it is in fact a warranty: see *Schuler AG* v *Wickman Machine Tools Sales Ltd*. Alternatively, where a breach of a term can have either a minor or major effect the courts tend to classify the term as innominate. If the breach is minor then only damages will be awarded: see *Hong Kong Fir Shipping Co. Ltd* v *Kawasaki Kisen Kaisha Ltd* [1962] 1 All ER 474. Answer [D] is incorrect. Smelly Perfume cannot repudiate for the reasons already stated and therefore will only be entitled to damages if any loss has been suffered.

26. [D] is the correct answer. [A] is correct. Provided there is sufficient evidence of a custom which is applicable to the contract the courts will apply it to a contract: see *Hutton* v *Warren* (1836) 1 M & W 466. [B] is correct. For example, the Sale of Goods Act 1979 implies several terms into contracts of sale. [C] is correct. The courts will imply a term by law where the contract is a recognisable type and an obvious gap needs filling: see *Liverpool City Council* v *Irwin* [1977] AC 239. [D] is, therefore, correct.

27. [D] is the correct answer. The issue is whether there is a repudiatory breach. *Hong Kong Fir Shipping Co. Ltd* v *Kawasaki*

Kisen Kaisha Ltd [1962] 2 QB 71 shows that the consequence of a breach is dependent on whether the innocent party has been deprived of a substantial benefit under the contract. Item (i) is probably less likely because in recent times a somewhat different approach has been adopted: see *Hong Kong Fir Shipping Co. Ltd.* Many contractual undertakings cannot be called 'conditions' or 'warranties'. Instead the proper approach is to examine the consequences of the breach. If the breach is disastrous the contract may be taken as terminated; if not disastrous only damages may be claimed: see *Cehave NV v Bremer* [1976] QB 44. Item (iii) is probably incorrect because the club have breached the contract at the time that the contract was due for performance; not before the time due for performance. It is, therefore, unlikely that the courts would find anticipatory breach: see *White & Carter (Councils) Ltd* v *McGregor* [1962] AC 413.

28. [C] is the correct answer. A mere representation is a statement of fact made before a contract is entered into but without the intention that it should induce the other party to enter into the contract. If the intention, when viewed objectively, indicates that the person making the statement did not intend it to induce the other party to enter into the contract, then the statement will amount to a mere representation. [A] is incorrect because this is the least likely answer. Mere puffs are statements which are so vague that they have no effect at law, or in equity; but there is liability for more precise terms: see *Carlill* v *Carbolic Smoke Ball Co.* [1893] 1 QB 256. [B] is incorrect because Ross does not warrant that the boat is perfect; he simply says it is a 'sound old tub'. Therefore, it is unlikely that this statement amounts to a warranty: see *Hopkins* v *Tanquerary* (1854) 15 CB 130. Also there is nothing to suggest that here the seller has special product knowledge as in *Dick Bentley Products Ltd* v *Harold Smith (Motors) Ltd* [1965] 1 WLR 623, so as to give rise to a warranty. [D] is incorrect because a statement will not be regarded as a term of the contract if the person making it expressly asks the other party to verify its truth: see *Ecay* v *Godfrey* (1947) 80 Ll L Rep 286.

29. [D] is the correct answer. Where a contract is reduced to writing, neither party can bring evidence to show there are other terms which are not in writing. This is the parole evidence rule. However, there are many exceptions to this rule. [A] is incorrect. If the contract is partially written and partially oral the rule does not apply: see *Jacobs* v *Batavia and General Plantations Trust* [1924] 1 Ch 287. [B] is incorrect. The rule does not apply to the validity of the contract (cf. intention and consideration): see *Kleinwort Benson* v *Malaysia Mining Corp.* [1988] 1 All ER 714. [C] is incorrect. The rule does not apply to implied terms: see *Gillespie Bros* v *Cheny, Eggar & Co.* [1896] 2 QB 59. [D] is therefore correct.

30. [D] is the correct answer. [A] is incorrect. This problem is similar to *Shell UK* v *Lostock Garage Ltd* [1977] 1 All ER 481. There are two broad categories of implied terms. Where the contract is of a common type and where the law is insufficient to define what the parties intended, it must be essential in order to make the contract work. This problem does not fall into that category. [B] is incorrect. The other category is where the parties intended there to be such a clause and it is necessary for business efficacy. The contract here can work without such an implied clause. [C] is incorrect. Clauses will not be implied unless they come within the above even if it would appear fair and reasonable to do so. [D] is therefore correct.

31. [D] is the correct answer because a misrepresentation must be of fact. [A] is incorrect because a statement of law cannot amount to a misrepresentation: see *Brikom Investments* v *Seaford* [1981] 1 WLR 863. [B] is incorrect because a statement of opinion does not usually amount to a misrepresentation: see *Bisset* v *Wilkinson* [1927] AC 177. *Note*: There are circumstances in which an opinion is construed as a statement of fact. For example, where the person giving the opinion was in a position to know the true facts and it can be proved that the person concerned could not reasonably have held such a view as a result, then in this situation the person's opinion will be treated as a statement of fact: see *Smith* v *Land House Property Corporation* (1884) 28 ChD 7. [C] is incorrect because statements of intention cannot amount to a misrepresentation. *Note*: The situation is different if the stated intention is not in fact held: see *Edgington* v *Fitzmaurice* (1885) 29 ChD 459.

32. [C] is the correct answer. Where one party, Goddard, makes an offer to another, Denning, and he, Goddard, is aware that that other party, Denning, is fundamentally mistaken as to the nature of the promise contained in his, Goddard's, offer the contract will be void for mistake: Goddard knows that he has offered 'old port' and also knows that Denning is fundamentally mistaken as to the terms of his offer since he thinks he is buying 'old vintage port'. The contract is therefore void for mistake: see *Hartog* v *Colin and Shields* [1939] 3 All ER 566. [A] and [B] are not correct because there has been no misrepresentation by Goddard. Denning has brought about his own misunderstanding and although Goddard will know that Denning is mistaken there is no duty on him to correct Denning's misunderstanding; silence is not a misrepresentation: see *Keates* v *The Earle of Cadogan* (1851) 10 CB 591. It follows that since Denning has the remedy provided for in option [C], [D] must be wrong.

33. [C] is the correct answer. [A] is not correct because although there has been no breach of contract Steve does have a remedy based on Emma's misrepresentation. [B] is not correct because although Steve might not have been very wise in not having the business's books checked he is under no duty to check the books: see *Central Rly Co. of Venezuela* v *Kisch* (1867) LR 2 HL 99. [C] is correct because Emma is guilty of a 'negligent' misrepresentation under s. 2 of the Misrepresentation Act 1967 because she did not have reasonable grounds for believing the facts that she represented were true; she had not bothered to check her facts: see *Howard Marine and Dredging Co. Ltd* v *Ogden and Sons (Excavations) Ltd* [1978] QB 574. [D] is incorrect first, because Steve will have lost his right to rescind the contract through lapse of time: see *Leaf* v *International Galleries* [1950] 2 KB 86; and secondly, the remedy of an indemnity is available only where the representee (Steve) has suffered a loss which was necessarily created by the contract; here no such loss has arisen: see *Whittington* v *Seale-Hayne* (1900) 82 LT 49.

34. [B] is the correct answer. The contract is void for mistake because unbeknown to both parties the commercial object of the hire no longer existed at the time of the party: see *Couturier* v *Hastie* (1856) 5 HLC 673. Answer [A] is incorrect. The contract is not frustrated. Frustration relates to events which occur after the contract was entered into, whereas this is to do with events before the contract is made: see *Taylor* v *Caldwell* (1863) 3 B & S 826. Answer [C] is incorrect. The contract is not enforceable because although it can be technically performed its commercial object did not exist at the time the contract was made.

35. [C] is the correct answer. This question is based upon the decision in *Bell* v *Lever Bros* [1932] AC 161. The severance contract is valid because at the time the parties entered into the agreement neither knew it could be severed without compensation. The mistake is not fundamental. It does not go to the root of the contract. Mistake as to quality is not generally sufficient to make a contract void. Answer [A] is incorrect. The contract is not void for mistake. The mistake is merely in respect of the quality of the service contract and is therefore not fundamental. Answer [B] is incorrect. The employment contract was voidable only until the severance contract was made. Answer [D] is incorrect. The contract is not frustrated. Frustration relates to events which occur after the contract was entered into, whereas this is to do with a mistake which occurred at the time the contract was made: see *Taylor v Caldwell* (1863) B & S 826.

36. [B] is the correct answer. An injunction is *unavailable* as a remedy for mistake. An injunction will only be granted to restrain a breach of contract if the clause which the plaintiff seeks to enforce is negative in substance: see *Warner Bros Pictures Inc. v Nelson* [1937] 1 KB 209. [A] is incorrect. A compromise may be imposed where the courts feel it is fair to do so: see *Solle v Butcher* [1950] 1 KB 671. [C] is incorrect. The court may refuse to order specific performance, as requested by a party (*x*) of party (*y*) where *x* is aware of *y*'s mistake when it was not induced by misrepresentation. [D] is incorrect. Rectification may be ordered where a document does not correctly reflect the intention of the parties: see *Joscelyne v Nissen* [1970] 2 QB 86.

37. [D] is the correct answer. Based on the current case law none of the above remedies would be available to Alex who has made a bad bargain. Item (i) is incorrect because it is not a strong possibility. Alex is unlikely to be able to invoke the assistance of equity in cases of common mistake: see *Solle v Butcher* [1950] 1 KB 671. Here there is little to suggest that equity should intervene: see *Riverplate Properties Ltd v Paul* [1975] Ch 133. Item (ii) is unlikely here since the case of *Bell v Lever Bros* [1932] AC 161 has confined operative mistake within very narrow lines. The case of *Associated Japanese Bank Ltd v Credit du Nord SA* [1988] 3 All ER 902 suggests that the occurrence of mistake as to quality rendering a contract void at common law is rare. Item (iii) is incorrect because there is no evidence of any representations having induced the contract. Item (iv) is incorrect because an injunction is only likely when a party has promised not to do something, such as selling the painting within 6 months of purchase.

38. [C] is the correct answer. Undue influence can be established if the party wanting to set aside the transaction can show that the other party influenced him to such an extent that he was dominated and entered into the contract as a consequence of this domination. If Tom can show that he reposed trust and confidence in Natasha to the extent it dominated him the transaction can be set aside: see *Tate v Williamson* (1866) LR 2 Ch App 55. Answer [B] is incorrect. In order to establish duress there must be actual threats. This did not occur here: see *The Siboen and The Sibotre* [1976] 1 Lloyd's Rep 293. Answer [D] is incorrect. In certain relationships there is a presumption of undue influence: see *Allcard v Skinner* (1887) 36 ChD 145. There is no such presumption between student and lecturer. It therefore follows that [A] is incorrect.

39. [A] is the correct answer. The *contra preferentum* rule applies to exemption clauses and states that words are strictly interpreted against the person relying on them. The clause only refers to persons and nothing else. The incident relates to an excessive load and not persons. The facts of the incident must fit within the narrow interpretation of the clause otherwise it will not protect: see *Houghton v Trafalgar Insurance* [1954] 1 QB 247. [B] is incorrect. The test of reasonableness at common law is not applicable. [C] is incorrect. Exclusion clauses are interpreted narrowly. [D] is incorrect. The *contra preferentum* rule is applicable to all contracts which incorporate an exclusion clause.

40. [D] is the correct answer. In *Chester Grovesnor Hotel Company Ltd v Alfred McAlpine Management Ltd* (1991) 56 BLR 115 it was held that where a party contracts on the same written terms without material variation those terms are deemed to be its standard form contract. However, if there are variations from the standard it does not mean it will fall outside the Unfair Contract Terms Act 1977. It is a question of fact whether the variations are to the extent that the contract can no longer be considered standard. Since Alpha Ltd made only minor changes to the contract, the contract will be considered to be made under DEF Ltd's standard written terms. [A] is incorrect. The 1977 Act applies to any standard written contract whether it is a consumer or commercial contract. [B] is incorrect. The contract has not been individually negotiated: see the explanation to option [D]. [C] is incorrect. Alpha Ltd will *not* be deemed to be acting as a consumer within the meaning of *R & B Customs Brokers Co. Ltd v*

United Dominions Trust Ltd [1988] 1 WLR 321 because the buying of computer hardware and software forms an integral part of their business.

41. [D] is *incorrect* and is the right answer. [A] is correct. The statutory implied terms cannot be excluded under the Unfair Contract Terms Act 1977 unless the party is not a consumer. In that situation, if the implied terms have been excluded, the test is one of reasonableness: see s. 6(3) of the Unfair Contract Terms Act 1977. [B] is correct. At common law if the clause adequately protects the party then the clause is valid: see *Photo Productions Ltd* v *Securicor Transport Ltd* [1980] 1 All ER 556. [C] is correct. If the party had notice of the clause before entering into the contract then it is incorporated into the contract: see *Thornton* v *Shoe Lane Parking* [1971] 2 QB 163. [D] is *incorrect*. When deciding whether a clause is reasonable the court looks at all the circumstances of the case along with the guidelines in sch. 2 of the Unfair Contract Terms Act 1977. The strength of bargaining power of the parties and notice of the clause are only two of the many factors which have to be considered when deciding whether the clause is reasonable. In addition, the court will consider the fact that the exclusion clause gives insufficient time to approve the goods. On this point the exclusion clause will be deemed unreasonable: see *RW Green Ltd* v *Cade Brothers Farms* [1978] 1 Lloyd's Rep 602.

42. [C] is the correct answer. This question is similar to the recent case of *St Albans District Council* v *International Computers Ltd* [1995] FSR 686. In deciding whether a clause is reasonable all the circumstances are considered including the effects of the clause on the respective parties. [A] is incorrect. A clause will not automatically be deemed valid simply because it is between two businesses who have signed the contract and had the opportunity to read it. [B] is incorrect. The Unfair Terms in Consumer Contracts Regulations 1994 do not apply to business contracts. It follows that [D] is incorrect.

43. [D] is the correct answer. The decision could no longer be repeated as terms that exclude liability for death or injury due to negligence in contracts such as the contract in *Thompson* v *London Midland and Scottish Rly* [1930] 1 KB 41 are now void by virtue of s. 2(1) of the Unfair Contract Terms Act 1977. [A] is incorrect because constructive notice of an exclusion clause has not been abolished. In law an assumption is made that the customer will (as in the *Thompson* case) have followed the directions on, say a ticket etc., as to where all the terms of the contract may be ascertained, and then have taken the trouble to read those terms, before entering the contract by retaining the ticket. Although this is a complicated approach taken to the communication of terms to the customer, how on the other hand can complicated terms be notified in a ticket type contract? [B] is incorrect because *non est factum* is a specialised form of defence to mistake whereby a party to a contract seeks to deny the contract on the grounds that 'it is not my deed': see *Saunders* v *Anglia Building Society* [1971] AC 1004. [C] is incorrect because the 1977 Act does not make such a clause unlawful but rather void from the beginning.

44. [C] is the correct answer. Of course if the new carrier's price was lower than Pear's price Apple would only be able to sue Pear for nominal damages so it would not be worth suing at all. [A] is wrong because only Pear anticipated that the goods would be transported via the tunnel so the common intention of both the parties has not been frustrated: see *Tsakiroglou and Co. Ltd* v *Noblee Thorl GmbH* [1962] AC 93. [B] is incorrect because the fact that Pear will now make a loss is irrelevant: see *Davis Contractors Ltd* v *Fareham UDC* [1956] 2 All ER 145 where Lord Radcliffe said '. . . it is not hardship or inconvenience or material loss itself which calls the principle of frustration into play'. [D] is incorrect because the market price is irrelevant in this type of situation; Apple's damages will be the difference between his agreed price with Pear and the price the new carrier charges him.

45. [A] is the correct answer. A frustrating event outside the control of the parties automatically brings the contract to an end: see *Hirji Mulji* v *Cheong Yue SS Co.* [1926] AC 497. A breach of a condition of a contract ([B]) on the other hand does not in itself bring the contract to an end; it merely gives the innocent party the right to accept the repudiatory breach and thus bring the contract to an end. The innocent party can choose to affirm the contract and continue with its performance: see *White and Carter (Councils) Ltd* v *McGregor* [1962] AC 413.

46. [C] is the correct answer. The sole purpose of the contract had ceased and therefore the contract was frustrated: see *Krell* v *Henry* [1903] 2 KB 740. [A] is incorrect. The contract is not frustrated because the concert is not the sole purpose of his visit to London: see *Herne Bay Steamboat Co.* v *Hutton* [1903] 2 KB 683. [B] is incorrect. The ship was in breach of contract since it had left Canada too late to perform the contract regardless of the frustrating event. [D] is incorrect. The work done was not that different to what was contemplated and therefore the delay was not enough to frustrate the contract: see *Tsakiroglou and Co. Ltd* v *Noble Thorl GmbH* [1962] AC 93.

47. [A] is the correct answer. A restraint must in fact be negative in substance for it to be enforced by an injunction. [B] is incorrect. An injunction will not be granted if its practical effect would be to compel the performance of a contract which is not specifically enforceable: see *Whitwood Chemical Co.* v *Hardman* [1891] 2 Ch 416. [C] is incorrect because the promise here is not negative in substance; but involves the enforcement of a positive promise. [D] is incorrect because although a contract may include a negative provision, an injunction will not be granted if its practical effect would be to compel the performance of a contract, which is not specifically enforceable: see *Chappell* v *Times Newspaper Ltd* [1975] 2 All ER 233.

48. [C] is the correct answer. The law protects the right to trade freely with goods, money and labour. [A] is incorrect. Any restriction or limitation is *prima facie* void to begin with: see *Greer* v *Sketchley* [1979] IRLR 455. This means that if restraint is unreasonable the contract, or at least part of it, remains in force. [B] is incorrect for the reasons given in [A]. [D] is incorrect as contracts in restraint of trade are not automatically valid.

49. [B] is the correct answer. Such clauses will be *prima facie* void where their only aim is to protect an employer from the competition of a previous employee. All employees should be given the opportunity to exercise their job skills: see *Morris* v *Saxelby* [1916] 1 AC 688 and *Attwood* v *Lamont* [1920] 2 KB 571. [A] is incorrect because an employer is entitled to protect his client lists when the employer has close links with his customers: see *Fitch* v *Dewes* [1921] 2 AC 158. [C] is incorrect because an employer is entitled to protect his trade secrets: see *Forster & Sons Ltd* v *Suggett* (1918) 35 TLR 87. [D] is incorrect because an employer is permitted to protect his trade marks.

50. [D] is the correct answer. [A] is incorrect because if an intervening event occurs which prevents total performance and is the fault of neither party the contract is frustrated. [B] is incorrect because the Law Reform (Frustrated Contract) Act 1943 does not have any such provision to share the loss equally between the parties. [C] is incorrect because under s. 1(2) of the Law Reform (Frustrated Contracts) Act 1943 expenses can only be reimbursed if a deposit was payable in advance. [D] is correct because the Law Reform (Frustrated Contracts) Act 1943 only applies to situations where either payment was due in advance or some benefit had been obtained by the other party. Under common law all liabilities under the contract cease at the time of the frustrating event. Payment was not due until the boiler was installed and therefore the frustrating event terminates liability: see *Appleby v Myers* (1867) LR 2 CP 651.

51. [A] is the correct answer. Quite clearly Arnold has made a repudiatory breach of contract by cancelling his order. However, Zed can only claim damages for the loss that flows naturally from Arnold's breach: see *Hadley v Baxendale* (1854) 9 Exch 341. Further, Zed is under a duty to mitigate his loss. This means, in this particular case, that Zed should have sought the best possible price for the SuperMan Rotavator which would have been £1,700. If Zed had done this he would have made an extra of £200 instead of the loss of £300 which he brought on himself: see *British Westinghouse Electric and Manufacturing Co. Ltd v Underground Electric Railways Co. of London Ltd* [1912] AC 673 where Haldane LC said that there is a principle '. . . which imposes on a plaintiff the duty of taking all reasonable steps to mitigate the loss consequent on the breach, and debars him from claiming in respect of any part of the damage which is due to neglect on his part'.

52. [D] is the correct answer. The courts make a distinction between liquidated damages clauses which are enforceable and penalty clauses which are not. In *Dunlop Pneumatic Tyre Co. Ltd v New Garage and Motor Co. Ltd* [1915] AC 79 the court laid down rules for determining whether a clause is a liquidated damages clause or penalty clause. If the amount of the clause is excessive compared with the actual loss then the clause is a penalty clause and unenforceable. [B] is incorrect. This will still be the case even if the clause only relates to one event: see *Dunlop Pneumatic Tyre Co. Ltd v New Garage and Motor Co.* [C] is incorrect. The Unfair Terms in Consumer

Contracts Regulations 1994 only applies to consumers. [A] is incorrect. Knowledge of the clause is not relevant in deciding whether it is enforceable.

53. [C] is the correct answer and will be enforced provided it is a pre-estimate of loss that flows from a breach of contract, or gives a pre-estimate of loss. The liquidated damages constitutes the amount, no more and no less, that the plaintiff is entitled to recover in the event of the breach without being required to prove actual damage: see *Wallis v Smith* (1882) 21 ChD 243. [A] is incorrect because this is a description of a penalty clause, and as such it will not be enforced if it holds a party in fear of breach contract: see *Dunlop Pneumatic Tyre Co. Ltd v Selfridge and Co. Ltd* [1915] AC 847. [B] is incorrect as in [A] as it is not a description of a liquidated damages clause. [D] is incorrect because an onerous clause in a contract is not a definition of a liquidated damages clause. *Note*: In *Public Works Commission v Hill* [1908] AC 368 Lord Dunedin refers to four tests to help distinguish between a penalty clause and a liquidated damages provision.

54. [A] is the correct answer. This problem is similar to *Ruxley Electronics and Construction Ltd v Forsyth* [1995] 3 All ER 268. Where there has been no loss of value and the cost of reinstatement is too high the courts will award a modest sum for loss of amenity. [B] is incorrect. The courts will not award the costs of reinstatement because the expense of the work involved would be out of all proportion to the benefit obtained. [C] is incorrect. Tom will obtain more than nominal damages. [D] is incorrect. The courts will not grant damages for both loss of pleasure and the cost of reconstruction.

55. [B] is the correct answer. A contract executed by deed is an exception to the rule requiring consideration. If the disposition is to be by way of gift no consideration passes and therefore it cannot be enforced by specific performance. Further equity 'will not assist a volunteer'. [A] is incorrect because a contract involving 'made to measure shoes' may be subject to such a remedy: see *Sky Petroleum v VIP Petroleum* [1974] 1 All ER 954. [C] is incorrect because only nominal damages could be awarded to the plaintiff where the defendant agreed to pay money to a third party. He will not be able to enforce it because of the doctrine of 'privity of contract'. [D] is incorrect because an order is often granted because of the individual and unique nature of land: see *Cohen* v *Roche* [1927] 1 KB 169.

56. [B] is the correct answer. Because neither Sandra and Paul had performed their obligations under the original contract both their considerations were executory. This being the case both parties can agree to forgo their rights under the contract in return for the other party forgoing their rights under the contract. In this way both parties furnish consideration in the second contract whereby they agree to abandon the original agreement. This is known as rescission: see *Foster* v *Dawber* (1851) 6 Exch 839. [A] is wrong because accord and satisfaction only arises where one of the parties has already performed their part of the bargain as, for example, where one party has already delivered goods to the other under the terms of a contract. [C] is wrong because the parties are not trying to vary the terms of the original contract but to abandon it altogether. [D] is wrong because neither party is purporting to waive a breach of contract of the other.

57. [D] is the correct answer because this is *not* one of the exceptions to the rule. This is a court order instructing one party to do what he has contracted to do. Specific performance will not be awarded where damages would be sufficient, nor will it be granted to enforce contracts for personal services: see *Page One Records* v *Britton* [1967] 3 All ER 822. [A] is incorrect because this is one of the exceptions to the harsh rule. A party who performs his obligations defectively but substantially can enforce the contract: see *Boone* v *Eyre* (1779) 1 Hy Bl 273n. [B] is incorrect because this is another exception to the harsh rule – if it can be shown, as in *Rithchie* v *Atkinson* [1808] 10 East 295, that particular parts of the contract are severable. [C] is incorrect because again this is an exception. If one party partially performs his obligation and the other accepts the work it may be possible to infer the parties have agreed to abandon the original contract: see *Christy* v *Row* (1808) 1 Taunt 300.

58. [A] is the correct answer. Nici's breach is an anticipatory breach of contract. She has made a repudiatory breach by telling Balti that she is cancelling her order. Balti is therefore entitled to sue as soon as Nici has made the repudiatory breach, i.e. immediately; there is no obligation on the innocent party, Balti, to wait until the date when the contract was due to be performed: see *Hochster* v *De La Tour* (1853) 2 E & B 678. It follows, therefore, that [B], [C] and [D] are wrong.

59. [A] is *incorrect* and is the right answer. Specific performance is an equitable remedy and is *not* automatically granted by the court: see *Nutbrown* v *Thornton* (1804) 10 Ves 159 and *Behnke* v *Bede Shipping* [1927] 1 KB 649. [B] is correct because this will always be an option open to the innocent party. The doctrine of anticipatory breach allows the victim to sue at once. The company does not have to wait until the time fixed for performance to arrive: see *Hochester* v *De La Tour* (1853) 2 E & B 678. [C] is correct because Speedy Travel can wait until the time of performance if they wish: see *Frost* v *Knight* (1872) LR 7 Exch 111. [D] is correct because all injured parties must do what they can to mitigate for breach of contract: see *White & Carter (Councils) Ltd* v *McGregor* [1961] 3 All ER 1178.

60. [D] is the correct answer for actions for breach of simple contract. [A] is incorrect because 2 years is not laid down by the Limitation Act 1980. [C] is incorrect for the same reason as in [A]. [B] is incorrect because 12 years relates to actions for breach of speciality contracts.

TITLES IN THE SERIES

Constitutional & Administrative Law
Contract
Company Law
Conveyancing
Wills and Probate
EC Law